MASSACHUSETTS
Treasures

MASSACHUSETTS
Treasures

A Guide to Marvelous, Must-See Museums

Chuck D'Imperio

BRIGHT LEAF
AMHERST AND BOSTON

An imprint of University of Massachusetts Press

Copyright © 2018 by University of Massachusetts Press
All rights reserved
Printed in the United States of America

ISBN 978-1-62534-372-7 (paper); 371-0 (hardcover)

Designed by Sally Nichols
Set in Berkeley Old Style and Zilla Slab
Printed and bound by Books International, Inc.

Cover design by Rebecca S. Neimark, Twenty-Six Letters
Cover photos: (top left) *Streamline engine at Chester Railway Museum,* photo
by Lee Snider/Deposit Photos; (top right) *Eternal Presence* sculpture by John
Wilson at the National Center of Afro-American Artists in Roxbury, photo by
Tim Saxton, https://creativecommons.org/licenses/by-sa/2.0/; (bottom left)
The Old Drum Shop from John Banks's Civil War blog, photo by John Banks,
https://john-banks.blogspot.com; (bottom right) *Boston Tea Party Ship* Eleanor,
photo by Melvyn Longhurst/Alamy Stock Photo.

Library of Congress Cataloging-in-Publication Data
A catalog record for this book is available from the Library of Congress.

British Library Cataloguing-in-Publication Data
A catalog record for this book is available from the British Library.

Unless otherwise noted, photographs have been taken by the author.

This book is dedicated to my friend and fellow journeyman, Mike Newell.

*Wherever you are, Mike,
I hope your mountains are blue.*

Contents

Region One: Northeast

Region Two: Greater Boston/Boston Metro

Region Seven: Berkshires

Foreword

I've long been interested in Massachusetts and have been through the state many times, with "been through" being the operative phrase. This book, written over the course of a year, has allowed me to spend more time here researching, traveling, interviewing, and visiting every corner of it. What a treasure trove of history this state contains! And that trove is reflected and presented in a number of its fascinating museums.

I believe that the final selection of forty-two museums for *Massachusetts Treasures* is a fair representation of the state as a whole. Of course, the book could have included a hundred and still not covered them all. Therefore, I kept the number on the small side, so as to better dig deeply into the personal connections of each of the museum's leaders, directors, managers, and staff. How did I come up with these forty-two? Well, as you will see, they are diverse, they are wide-ranging, and they cover smaller, "unknown" museums and collections, as well as including some Massachusetts museums that are among the most popular in the state. Also, these entries geographically cover the entire state from end to end—from the Gilded Age Museum in the Berkshires to the French Cable Station Museum on Cape Cod, to Hammond Castle Museum in Gloucester, to Battleship Cove in Fall River, and to several located in the Boston area. A little bit of something for everybody.

We recognize that almost everyone is familiar with, say, the John F. Kennedy Museum and Presidential Library in Boston. But that many might not be familiar with the JFK Hyannis Museum on Cape Cod. So we included it. We also recognize the fact that the Norman Rockwell Museum in the west and the Museum of Fine Arts in Boston in the east each welcome tens of thousands of visitors annually. But the Museum of Bad Art in Somerville could use a little help. Se we made our decisions carefully.

Many of the museums in this book are out of the way, unheard-of, and unique. Some are mere private collections for which the owner has spent a lifetime researching and archiving. Some are a bit pricey to get into, and a surprising number of them are free. The smaller ones are the most fun. The Paper House. The *Titanic* Museum. The Beer Can Museum. The Massachusetts State Police Museum. The National Black Doll Museum. See what I mean? They are all wonderful.

Known or unknown, big or small, the purpose of this book is to get you, the reader, out of your chair and into your car to visit each one of them. They are all fascinating, and through the interviews in this book you will see that they all have very interesting backstories. This book is simply meant to tease the reader to hit the road and find out more.

Each chapter is presented so you can easily find all the pertinent visitor information, read my own take on the museum, enjoy the narrative of the history of the museum directly from the administrative staff, and create a personal itinerary of other nearby museums. A section titled "Up around the Bend" is included so you are aware of some other places of interest nearby, whether it be a historic village or even a popular tourist stop or restaurant.

Most important is a special section called the "Wow Factor." This is the section that I believe really sets this book apart from all other Massachusetts travel guides. I personally visited each of the museums in the book, and during those visits I set aside a significant amount of private time to interview their directors. I walked the museum floors with them, listened carefully to their personal stories and their connections with the subject matter, and marveled at their passion and commitment to their work. At the end of each visit I asked them to describe their personal wow factor in their museum. What was the one item in the collection that really struck a chord with them, an artifact that was, in their opinion, an extra-special item or one that gave them pause or, sometimes, caused them to tear up with emotion? I think you will agree that their answers are quite thoughtful, remarkable, and surprising.

It is rare to find such a large number of museum directors and administrators on the record with their own personal thoughts about their museums in a single book. For that, I believe that *Massachusetts Treasures* is unique.

The range of museums highlighted in this book is extensive. Birthplaces? Yes, those of two legendary American women. An entertainment museum that counts among its artifacts an authentic Academy Award statue for the museum owner? Yes, in Lee. A tiny house that was deemed so important to our national defense that the U.S. Marines guarded it around the clock during World War I? Yes, in Orleans. A small yet engrossing museum dedicated to the doomed ocean liner *Titanic*? Yes, in the back room of Henry's Jewelry Store in Indian Orchard. A little undervisited museum to a U.S. president with ties to the Bay State *not* named Kennedy or Adams? Yes, on the second floor of a public library in western Massachusetts. A museum and drum factory where they've made percussion instruments for Paul McCartney as well as a drum for Abraham Lincoln's funeral? Yes, in Granville. Or, how about a museum that is basically a forest owned by one of the world's great seats of learning? Yes, in central Massachusetts, just fifteen miles south of the New Hampshire border.

There are treasures around every corner in this beautiful state. And you will find them in the many museums, both big and small, that are out there just waiting for you to visit them so you can learn the stories for yourself.

Happy travels.

Chuck D'Imperio
Unadilla, N.Y.

Author's Note

When using this book as a guide to your travels, it is important that you always call ahead or search out the museum's website. Some may close, move, or change hours with little notice.

Map of the Regions of Massachusetts

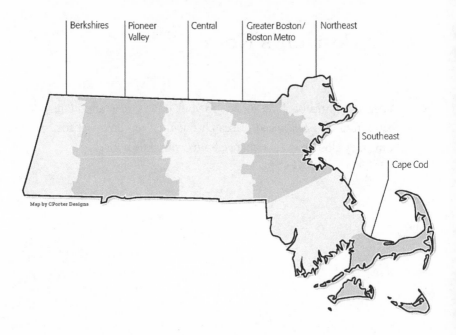

Berkshires

Pioneer
Valley

Central

Greater Boston/
Boston Metro

Northeast

Southeast

Cape Cod

Map by CPorter Designs

MASSACHUSETTS
Treasures

REGION ONE
Northeast

Hammond Castle Museum, 80 Hesperus Ave, Gloucester (493814), photograph by Robert Linsdell. Creative Commons license available at: https://creativecommons.org/licenses/by/2.0/.

1 Hammond Castle Museum

Gloucester

On my most recent visit to the Hammond Castle Museum, I caught Linda Rose, the events director, at a very busy time. The gift shop was packed with customers, the parking lot was full, a large queue of tourists was lined up to go through the castle, and staff were preparing a big wedding on the castle lawn overlooking the ocean.

"Yes, we do stay busy here," she said. We sat for a few quiet moments in her office far above the maddening crowd. "This place has so many wonderful attributes to it. Its beauty, its story, its location, its history. It is really quite remarkable. You will see all kinds of amazing things along your tour. The castle was built by John Hays Hammond, Jr. He was a prolific inventor and electronics pioneer.

He was known as 'The Father of the Remote Control' and had hundreds of patents to his name. He built this dream castle of his on this beautiful bluff overlooking our harbor. And, as you will see, he was an untiring collector."

Hammond Castle is intimidating. Built in the mid-1920s, it incorporates all of the Middle Ages castle accoutrements one would expect. Every box is checked: warrens of dark, secret rooms, huge oil paintings, mosaic tile floors, wrought iron gates, arched entranceways, medieval torch sconces, period furniture, sprawling wall tapestries, European religious icons, gleaming suits of armor, stone statuary, false doors, a stained glass window opening up to a "Romeo and Juliet" balcony, a blacksmith shop, ancient weapons of war, a drawbridge (sorry, no moat), grand pianos, winding staircases, ornate chandeliers, massive stone fireplaces, and more. There is even a human skull in a box! I was told that the skull was that of an actual crew member with Christopher Columbus.

The Great Hall of the castle is one hundred feet long, sixty-five feet tall, and could comfortably seat ninety people for dinner. With stone walls, wrought-iron adornments, hanging battle flags, and high, arched windows, it appeared to be something lifted right out of an old Errol Flynn–Basil Rathbone swashbuckler. The hulking stone fireplace was not used. It wasn't needed. Hammond invented radiant floor heat. Later, the room was used to show first-run Hollywood films. The eccentric Mr. Hammond, a bit of a scamp in his day, would even hold lively Monopoly games here. The contestants played with real money and were allowed to take home any winnings.

Yes, every box is checked.

Wow Factor

"There is a bit of a wow factor in almost every room," Rose said. "But, I have to admit. I am a little partial to the courtyard. It is filled with stunning flowers, which surround Mr. Hammond's pool. Two-stories above, a glass greenhouse roof allows light to shine through. This kept the pool warm all year long. He was known to plunge into the pool at any given moment, sometimes fully dressed!

"Mr. Hammond created a 'weather system' for this room and he could make it rain with just the click of a switch inside the courtyard. Around the inside perimeter are four small storefronts which reflect the kind of buildings you would see in a rural French village. Each has elaborate carved imagery on the front. They are a winery, a farm store, a butcher shop, and a bakery. The entranceway to the courtyard from the Great Hall is made of volcano lava from Mount Etna. The Hammond's bedroom overlooked the courtyard. It is quite peaceful and beautiful."

The Takeaway

I could list my favorite things about Hammond Castle over several pages of this book. But for me, four stick out as really spectacular. In the Great Hall is one of America's rare pipe organs. It was made expressly for Hammond and has been played over the years by many of the great organists of his era, including the legendary Virgil Fox. It is said that this pipe organ is the largest single organ ever placed in a private residence. I did find it curious, however, that Hammond has no familial connection at all to the world-famous Hammond musical instrument company.

In the courtyard we find another manifestation of Mr. Hammond's whimsical nature. Late in life he ordered a life-sized statue of himself for the front lawn of the castle. The bronze statue, of a forever thirty-four-year-old, totally naked Hammond graced the grounds much to the embarrassment of his wife. She had his private parts covered with a bronze fig leaf, which has been the target of souvenir hunters over the years. Today, the statue stands in all its glory in the courtyard overlooking the pool.

The last room on the tour is the Invention Room. Many examples and artifacts of Hammond's prolific career as an inventor and engineer are on display here. Be sure to inspect the wall timeline of his inventions. "The Boy Inventor" is credited with hundreds of them. Examples include "System for Firing Torpedoes (10–3–1922)," "Castings for Musical Instruments (7–30–1929)," "Gas Tank for Airplanes (4–28–1936)," "Electric Shaver (10–21–1941)," and "Submarine Mines (1–2–1923)."

And then there is the Cushing Bedroom. This elaborate guest bedroom also overlooks the courtyard. The floors are made of bricks from one of Christopher Columbus's castles in Spain. In an adjoining room there is a secret passageway, which can only be found by pressing on the correct flower in the busy floral-patterned wallpaper. To call a servant, the guest would simply have to reach out from the bed and push a mother-of-pearl button hidden on the wall and a maid or cook would come scampering up the backstairs to answer the visitor's every need. The room is named after Richard Cardinal Cushing, the famous leader of the Roman Catholic archdiocese of Boston, who spent many summers here. A life-sized bronze bust of the cardinal stands on a windowsill in the room. Upon his death, the childless Hammond willed the castle to Cardinal Cushing and the church. When costs of upkeep became too much for the church, the castle was sold to a frequent guest on the property, organist Virgil Fox. It later became the Hammond Castle Museum.

Hammond was a cat lover and had as many as a dozen at one time. He died in 1965 at the age of seventy-six. He is buried on the grounds of Hammond Castle, just outside the drawbridge. His cats are buried with him.

The Nuts and Bolts

Hammond Castle Museum

80 Hesperus Avenue
Gloucester, Massachusetts 01930
(978) 283-2080
www.hammondcastle.org
This museum is not handicapped accessible.

Travel Suggestion

The castle is located five miles south of Gloucester's
Stacy Esplanade, a popular harbor-side boardwalk.

Museum Hours

May through June 11: Saturday to Sunday, 10 a.m. to 4 p.m.
June 12 through October 6: Tuesday to Sunday,
10 a.m. to 4 p.m.
Closed holidays

Admission

Adults: $12.00
Seniors (65+): $10.00
Children (6–12): $9.00

Up around the Bend

Gloucester is one of New England's great seaport towns and offers
much in the way of history, fine dining, and shopping venues.

2 The Paper House

Rockport

Hmmmm. Where to start?

First, yes this is a house. Made entirely out of paper.

Now, for the details. Located in the tiny hamlet of Pigeon Cove, just north of Rockport, this house is one man's fantasy house, yes, an obsessive fantasy, but a house nonetheless. Front porch, living room, fireplace, furniture, eating area, lamps, beds, chairs, shelving all made out of newspapers. And the curtains, too!

"I will agree, it is a little odd," Edna Beaudoin told me. She is the current owner of the Paper House and the great-niece of the builders, Elis and Esther Stenman. "They started it in 1922. They were from Sweden, and they were very frugal. Elis was an engineer and designer. He just one day decided to start constructing this house out of rolled-up newspapers. And he did," she said.

The house is a wonderment. The papers (both on the interior and exterior) are slathered in a heavy lacquer to preserve them. Still, little pieces do fall off.

"Oh, yes, sometimes even large chunks fall off," Beaudoin told me as she pointed to a discolored section of the front porch. "We had some water damage from that one. But, all in all, knock on, well, paper, the house is still pretty sturdy. My biggest concern is from all of the visitors who come through having a desire to touch the papers out of curiosity. I thought the problem might be from all the kids who visit. But really, I do have to watch the adults more. I finally had to put up a sign."

I noticed that sign on the front door: "Please resist the urge to touch. This house is 90 years old and is very fragile. The varnished paper is very brittle so *please keep your hands in your pockets!*"

The newspaper walls are plastered with large amounts of spar varnish, the same type of heavy-duty covering used to waterproof old wooden ships. Still, despite the dark discoloring and the age of the paper, headlines and advertisements are clearly visible. I noticed one headline that said, "24,000 See Red Sox Lose!" (*Boston Globe,* April 15, 1924). Another read, "Ellsworth Dam Ripped by Flood: Torn Away with a Roar Heard for Miles" (May 3, 1923). Another newspaper panel features an advertisement for a used Ford automobile: "$1.00 Down."

The outside walls of the house are less than one inch thick. The roof is made of wooden shingles. There are many pieces of furniture throughout the two-room abode. While Beaudoin was taking me through the house, a chair spindle just fell off and rolled across the living room floor.

"Oh, good," she laughed. "Now I can show you how they rolled the papers."

She held up the errant paper rail and showed me the inside. A piece of wire, to make it firm, went through the entire center of the tube, and then several large sheets of newspaper were wound around the wire until it was thick and secure. It was then placed on the furniture. Dozens of individual pieces of newspaper were used for just a single spindle or armrest.

"We estimate that well over 100,000 full newspapers were used to create this home."

The lamps are wired and work. A six-foot-tall grandfather clock keeps perfect time and is a highlight of the Paper House.

"It was their pride and joy. Mr. Stenman made the clock out of newspapers from every state capital in the United States. You can count them if you'd like. But remember, there were only 48 states back then," Beaudoin observed. And sure enough, there they were. All with the mastheads facing out. Papers from Albany, Sacramento, Lansing, Annapolis, Phoenix, and more.

There are chairs, a roll-top desk, a bed, and other home items scattered throughout the house. A huge corner fireplace (made of paper but nonworking) with a wide mantelpiece anchors one corner of the house. Sitting on the fireplace is a large, colorful double portrait of Elis and Esther. The caption under the portrait reads, "Elis F (age 20) and Esther M (age 20) Stenman. 1896 engagement photo." The large mantel is made up entirely of rolled up copies of the Boston *Sunday Herald* and the *New York Herald Tribune* color rotogravure sections.

I asked Beaudoin what intrigues people the most about this unusual little house. "They like to ask if the whole house is made of paper. And of course it is not. It wouldn't be here for almost a century if it was. It was built with a wooden frame and a wood roof. But, everything else is paper. There is a real working piano in the parlor area, but it too is completely covered with newspapers. They were very eccentric people, I guess. They were smart, too. He liked to employ themes for his paper furniture. For example, the writer's desk is made up of newspapers that tell of Lindbergh's

1927 flight to France. His bookcase is made up of *Christian Science Monitor* newspapers, which tell of important international affairs. I don't know whether this place is historical or hysterical, but it came to be mine and I really love this house."

Wow Factor

"Well, people like the six-foot-tall grandfather clock the most. But for me, my favorite item here is the rocking chair in the front sitting room. It is just so sentimental. I can just imagine Esther sitting in that chair rocking away as her husband was in the other room rolling up newspapers. It is charming. It was hers. I sat it in long ago. It was not very comfortable. But it is cute. And very special to me. And, it is made entirely out of rolled up papers!"

The Takeaway

This is one of those museums that you have to experience to understand. Try and explain a paper house to someone. It is nearly impossible. But, as Beaudoin said, the house has a lot of charm to it. One can imagine the Stenmans coming here for a weekend (it was mostly a summer cottage to them) and setting about their tasks of creating more paper furniture. It took them twenty years to complete. Madness is a word that nudges its way into my thoughts at the Paper House. But I resist that and will dub it "eccentric" instead. Certainly, this is one of the most unusual museums I have ever been to. And many others come here also. About two thousand visitors make their way up Pigeon Hill Street to the house every year.

Before I left, I perused the sign-in guestbook. Previous to my visit, the most recent visitors were from Pasadena, Maryland; Exeter, New Hampshire; Asheville, North Carolina; San Diego; and Bilbao, Spain!

The Nuts and Bolts

The Paper House

52 Pigeon Hill Street
Rockport, Massachusetts 01966
(978) 546-2629
www.paperhouserockport.com
This museum is not handicapped accessible.

Travel Suggestion

From the south: Take Route 128 North to Gloucester.
Turn left onto 127 North at the signal light. Follow 127 for
six miles. Turn left at the Pigeon Cove Post Office on to
Curtis Street and follow the signs to the Paper House.

Museum Hours

April through October: Daily, 10 a.m. to 5 p.m.

Admission

Adult: $2.00
Children: $1.00
Admission is on the honor system (a box is located
in the living room). Photos are allowed.
Note: This is a "self-guided" museum. It is usually
unattended, but Edna Beaudoin lives in the neighboring
house and will come out and chat with you about the
house and her ancestors if she sees you coming.

Up around the Bend

The dramatic Gloucester Fisherman's Memorial Statue, located
on the curving beach boardwalk of nearby Gloucester, is one of
the most photographed icons of the region. It is eight feet tall and
was dedicated in 1925.

3 New England Quilt Museum

~~~~~~

Lowell

This museum is a virtual kaleidoscope of dazzling colors, swirling patterns, and brilliant craftsmanship.

"We believe that we have the most comprehensive collection of quilts and quilting information available anywhere in New England," Nora Burchfield told me. She is the executive director of the New England Quilt Museum. "Our quilts are among the finest you will find on display in the country."

The museum occupies a unique corner spot in the Lowell National Historic District. The building was constructed by Josiah Peabody in the 1840s as the home of the Lowell Institute for Savings bank building. The facade of the building still carries the original bank's name. "We purchased this building over 20 years ago, and it just suits us perfectly," Burchfield observed. "Because it was built as a bank, we have a lot of display space and many unusual little areas. And there are two original bank vaults in the building."

I asked Burchfield what do they do with the vaults?

"We use them to store quilts, of course," she said.

The ground floor of the Quilt Museum is filled with display racks and cases, quilt samples, work areas, and items for sale. During my recent visit, the front door never stopped opening, with quilting aficionados coming in for supplies, books, or ideas. The second floor is reached by a large winding staircase or elevator. This is where the magic happens.

The gallery floor is a beautiful, large display area with several smaller galleries around the perimeter. The colors of the walls are muted, the lighting is dramatic, and the quilts on display are professionally presented. The room is host to an ever-changing series of exhibitions. The day I was at the museum they were displaying award-winning quilts from Japan.

"Just look at the hand quilting," Burchfield said as she encouraged me to move closer to one mammoth wall-covering quilt. "Look at the detail. This is an example of some of the finest quilt-making in the world today," she noted as we both leaned in to view the minute pattern of intricate designs that covered the quilt.

"All of these were created by the Master Quilters of Japan. People have come from all over to see these works of art." The one we were looking at was done by Miki Yakita. She is one of the premier quilt-makers in Japan.

"One thing that I really like about these quilts is the fact that no matter how elaborate, how elegant, or how sophisticated the design, they all adhere to the common core principals of quilt-making, which haven't changed in centuries. It has to have a top, a bottom, and a layer of filling in the middle with a running stitch that goes through all three layers.

"You must remember that even in previous centuries, quilts were not made for the sole purpose of keeping people warm. Quilts were used to make a statement. People made them to show off their creativity or their talents. An especially elaborate quilt might even be displayed to reflect one's wealth. They were pieces of art. Not to be touched or used for a common purpose. Many think we Americans came up with the whole art of quilt-making, like the Amish of Pennsylvania for instance. But we inherited our quilting heritage from our English ancestors."

Burchfield is a lively, passionate supporter of fiber arts. She has always had an interest in history and textiles so she is a good fit for this beautiful museum. "It is a marriage of sorts," she told me. "Women's history and art come together here. And it is natural that this museum is in Lowell. This was the birthplace of the American Industrial Revolution, and it was predominately women who wove the fabrics and created the textiles in all the old brick mills which line our landscape."

Lowell experienced a severe downturn in the 1970s, when many of the mills closed and the economy disappeared. It was under the guidance of then Massachusetts senator Paul Tsongas that so much federal money came in to reinvent and revitalize a new, vibrant historical center of the city.

"We say his name with great reverence around Lowell," Burchfield said in reference to Senator Tsongas. "Just look around at the rejuvenated downtown and historical corridor. We are so proud of what has happened, and we are excited for the city's future. The Quilt Museum is perfectly positioned to be an important part of Lowell's ongoing cultural Renaissance."

Wow Factor

For her museum wow factor, Burchfield took me into the Dono-
hue Gallery just off the main exhibit floor to show me her favorite
quilt. This space is dedicated to quilts in the museum's permanent
collection.

"As you can see, this quilt is a massive achievement," she said.
The quilt we were standing in front of covers an entire wall. It is
93 x 74 inches and was completed in 1865. "This quilt has many
qualities that make it extraordinary. Clearly this quilt-maker was
not an expert, but she was very creative."

The quilt is titled "Lemoyne Star Wedding Quilt," and it was
made by Penelope Carpenter Stanley as a wedding gift for her son
and his bride. It is mesmerizing.

"First of all we notice the sheer size of the quilt. It must have
taken this woman at least several months to complete. But what a
labor of love this was," Burchfield observed. "Look at all the little
idiosyncratic nuances to it. Of course we will never know why
these images were placed on the quilt, so we can only surmise.
And that is part of the fun of this quilt."

Splayed across this neutral tone quilt we can spot American
flags, hearts, a chicken sitting on a basket, anchors, flowers, and
more. In fact, each time you review the quilt it seems as if another
icon on it pops up.

"The hand quilting and applique work on this quilt is just
incredible. Remember, no machine ever touched this quilt. The
person who made this made it with love to give as a gift. We see
text stitched in small threads scattered around the quilt. One section reads, 'For Jerome and Ida, November 17, 1864.' We know
who they were. Jerome Henry Stanley married Ida M. Livenberger
and both were from New York City. They were a part of the wave
of immigrants who moved to Southern California in the 1870s.

In 1875, they owned an orange ranch in Redlands. So we know a lot about the people who received this quilt. But not much is known about the woman who made it.

"It is just an astonishing work. The maker used no fancy tools or equipment to create it. Imagine the tedium of cutting, arranging, and then stitching the hundreds of appliques on it. Just think of a mother, working endless hours to give this very special gift to her beloved son on his wedding day. It is so precious. I love this quilt and the sentiment it represents."

The Takeaway

Going into the Quilt Museum I had virtually no knowledge of quilts or how they were made. Honestly, I still do not. But I do know beauty and art when I see it, and this place is overflowing with both.

When cresting the top of the stairs of the museum and seeing the large exhibit space for the first time, it is not a stretch to say that a peaceful feeling washed over me. Viewing these enormous pieces of colorful textiles, and learning all of the backstories that each brings to the experience, can be transformative. On the day I was there I was completely swept up by the beauty and majesty of not only these magnificent art quilts that had traveled all the way from Japan to Lowell but also the many American items in the permanent collection.

It is hard to fathom how these quilts were made, unless you are an artisan. It is confounding, the exactitude and precision. But the results are so rewarding to view.

Visitors of all ages will enjoy it here. And men, take it from me, do not be afraid of this museum. It will surprise you.

The Nuts and Bolts

New England Quilt Museum

18 Shattuck Street
Lowell, Massachusetts 01852
(978) 452-4207
www.nequiltmuseum.org
This museum is handicapped accessible.

Travel Suggestion

Take advantage of the free parking at the nearby Lowell
National Historical Park Visitor Center. This is just a
couple of blocks from the Quilt Museum and is a good
place to start any visit to the historic district. They have
a well-stocked gift shop representing all of the major
Lowell attractions and also show a free video on the
history of Lowell.

Museum Hours

January through April: Tuesday to Saturday,
10 a.m. to 4 p.m.
May through December: Tuesday to Sunday,
10 a.m. to 4 p.m.

Admission

Adults: $9.00
Children under 12: Free

Up around the Bend

Over the years, Lowell has transformed its downtown into a highly
walkable area. The visitor center can provide you with a walking
tour map as well as suggestions for dining in the area. One could
easily spend a day visiting the historical sites of Lowell.

4 National Streetcar Museum at Lowell

〜✦〜

Lowell

Although the National Streetcar Museum is housed in a relatively anonymous looking brick building in Lowell's historic district, there are a few giveaways about what is inside. And they are big ones. Out front sit several old locomotives, streetcars, and steam engines harking back to Lowell's glory days as a major Massachusetts transportation hub.

"We had streetcars running all over town at one time," Paul Castiglione told me. Castiglione, age seventy-three when I met him, is the curator of this small but interesting museum. "Here we try and promote the use of light rail and street car lines wherever possible. This museum tells the streetcar story in several different ways," he said as he guided me around the museum.

The museum is small but packed with displays, artifacts, and

videos of the glory days of Massachusetts streetcars. "We have four streetcars here. Four trolleys—two of them are replicas of 1906 open cars, one was built using the blueprints of a 1914 closed car—and then we have our pride and joy, a 1924 New Orleans streetcar." The New Orleans car is the only one owned outright by the museum; the other three are owned by the National Park Service.

"The New Orleans car has a remarkable story to it," Castiglione said. "When we first found it, it was a complete mess. It needed a total refurbishing. We spent over $50,000 just on getting this single car restored in pristine condition. It originally was Streetcar 966, and it ran along Canal Street in New Orleans. It was one of the streetcars which inspired Tennessee Williams's *Streetcar Named Desire*. In fact, her sister car still rides the rails of New Orleans. Now 'old 966' is here, and it is stunning. We give rides on it on weekends when the weather is nice, and people just love it."

Paul Castiglione is obviously infatuated with the whole history of streetcars.

"Yes, I am. And it all started a long time ago when I was a young boy. When I was just four years old I got my first Lionel train set from my grandfather. Soon after I got ill and had to start making routine trips to Boston for medical appointments. These trips just reinforced my love for trains. We would pull into Boston late at night and I would look out of the window and see these giant machines charging through the black evening landscape. Steam was billowing from their locomotives and trolley cards zig-zagged all over the place with dazzling sparks flying off the wires overhead. It was very exciting.

"Streetcars left Lowell in 1935. A friend of mine and I took a ride out to the Seashore Trolley Museum in Kennebunkport, Maine. It is about eighty miles away. We pulled in, and there they were; dozens of these wonderful old streetcars. And I was hooked."

"That must have been quite a thrill for an enthusiast like you to see for the first time," I commented.

"If you remember that scene in the movie *Jurassic Park* where the scientist first sets his eyes upon all those dinosaurs, well, that was me," Castiglione recalled. "I began volunteering at the Streetcar Museum in 1959, and I am still a part of it."

Wow Factor

Castiglione's wow factor surprised me. "It's these little things right here," he said as he pointed to a glass case along a front wall. Inside was a collection of streetcar ephemera, some of it over a century old.

"Just think of it. These things were never made to last. Never. They were made out of flimsy paper and basically were designed just to be used and then discarded. The fact that we have so many of these items is amazing to me," he said.

The collection includes colorful old timetables, trolley schedules, tickets, and more. Some of them sport fancy artwork. There are several original vintage signs in the case ("Spitting is forbidden within the station"). The exhibit also holds old timeclocks, miniature models of streetcars, an old conductor's uniform, and fare tokens.

The Takeaway

This museum is small and can be easily toured in about an hour. It is best to visit on a day when your museum tour can be complimented with a streetcar ride on the rails out front.

Still, there are a few charming aspects to the museum. I particularly like the video presentations. One monitor shows a loop of film showing streetcars in the past in the Lowell area as well as around the country. One film shows a ride through San Francisco before the earthquake in 1906. The videos are in black and white; they are interesting and some are quite humorous. One, titled *Rube in the Subway,* shows some poor guy on his first trip into the city on a streetcar, getting fleeced in all sorts of manner by the slick city folks.

My favorite one, however, is a demonstration video made by a streetcar company showing a brand-new addition to its trains, the cow catcher. These were the fanned out metal "scoops" that (in theory) would move a cow gently off the tracks so the train could pass.

In this video, the inventors are showing off this new invention to a crowd of onlookers. The manufacturers had one big problem though: no cows. So, in lieu of cows being thrown aside, they used humans! It is hilarious to see the approaching streetcar coming down the tracks, and just as it gets in front of the crowd, some poor employee of the cow-catcher company actually flings himself onto the tracks where upon the cow catcher roughly scoops up the poor lad and pushes him out of the way.

It is really funny.

The Nuts and Bolts

National Streetcar Museum at Lowell

25 Shattuck Street
Lowell, Massachusetts 01852
(978) 458-5835
https://trolleymuseum.org/national-streetcar-museum
-lowell
This museum is handicapped accessible.
Note: This is a satellite museum to the much larger and
older Seashore Trolley Museum in Kennebunkport, Maine.

Travel Suggestion

This museum is located in the heart of the Lowell
National Historical Park District. You can park nearby
and visit many of the other museums and historic
buildings in this district, which are all close. A large
visitor's center is across the street from the Streetcar
Museum. Here you will find an extensive museum store
carrying gifts and souvenirs from each of the historic
venues in the district. The center also shows a
well-done, free fifteen-minute film telling the story
of Lowell's industrial past.

Museum Hours

May through October: Weekends, 11 a.m. to 4 p.m.

Admission

$3.00

Up around the Bend

With the Lowell historic area right at your feet, there are plenty
of interesting things to see and do, all within a couple of blocks
of this museum. Guided walking tour maps are available at the
visitor's center.

5 Boott Cotton Mills Museum

～～

Lowell

Tall, block-long empty brick buildings standing mute and watching over a changing landscape are not an unusual sight in the Northeast. As mill after mill closed down and left for more fertile grounds, these ghosts remain, marking the skylines of once thriving, industrious cities like Adams, Fall River, and Brockton, Massachusetts, and stretching westward across a rust swath into cities like Troy, Amsterdam, and Utica, New York. These communities now deal with these vacant reminders of the well-off past in a variety of ways. None, in my opinion, deals with it as successfully as Lowell.

The city, the fourth largest in the state, was one of the major manufacturing mill cities in the East a hundred years ago. Today many of these buildings have been turned into business complexes,

retail centers, residential towers, and office buildings. There are still many more old brick buildings to go, but the city seems to be onto something.

The Boott Cotton Mills Museum is a perfect example. This former textile manufacturing plant, once one of the largest factories in the United States, sat empty for years, long after the last company whistle blew in 1955. It had done yeoman's duty for well over a century here but ultimately succumbed to outside interests and changing business patterns, much like the fate of almost all mills in New England.

"This was a great mill. It employed thousands of workers, many of them young women in the beginning, and this museum tells an exciting and important story of America and the industrial revolution," Resi Polixa told me. She is a National Park ranger and interpreter at the mill museum. She was an excellent guide for my afternoon spent at Boott Mills.

First, the size. In a word, cavernous. "Not all the buildings on our campus are open to the public, but we have some of the most important ones up and open and staffed for visitors."

I asked her where we should start our tour, and she cheerily said, "At the beginning, of course." With this she guided me from the reception room, around the corner, and into the Weave Room. At first we stood behind plate glass and observed the enormous manufacturing floor in front of us. The size, scope, and sheer magnitude of what I was seeing was hard to comprehend.

"This Weave Room was the heart of Boott Mills. In here are between ninety and one hundred old operating mechanical looms. This is where hundreds of workers, in around the clock shifts, would produce the famous 'Lowell Cloth,' a generic name for the thousands of tons of cloth material produced here over the years."

I peered through the glass. Each machine was operating, clunking along, weaving plates shushing back and forth, wheels turning, everything moving. It seemed as if the room was alive. Underneath this window were display plaques with written testimonials from some of the thousands of workers who operated these very machines.

One of them read, "In the 'Weave Room' we had no ear protection at all. I still have trouble with my ears. I went to a doctor and told him I can't hear good. He asked me where I worked. I said, 'the Weave Room at Boott.' He looked at me and said, 'Oh, then just forget about it. I can't do nothing for you. These looms bang bang banged all day long. It gets in your ears, but you can't get it out.' John Falante, 1985."

After a short narration, Polixa took me inside the room. With no ear protection. The machines were loud, the room smelled sickly of oil, and it got very claustrophobic very quickly. Despite it being nearly the size of a football field, the room, with its hundred huge moving machines packed tightly next to each other, seemed way too small to handle the output of the mill in its heyday. Although all the machines were "bang bang banging" away, to use Mr. Falante's words, there were only four workers on the floor.

"Yes, we only use a couple of workers a day. They are making Lowell Cloth for us to sell in our museum store at the end of the tour." I waved to the workers. They looked up, ear plugs dangling from their necks, and waved back.

The second floor is the full museum. Here are more machines, a large number of photographic exhibits, numerous informational plaques, and several television monitors.

"These monitors play endless loops of oral histories from our former employees," I was told.

And here, inside these little video boxes, lies the real story of Boott Mills. The stories are incredible, border on the unbelievable, and are many times quite emotional.

Wow Factor

I asked the park ranger what her wow factor was. Her answer was profound.

She took me to a giant wall near the end of the tour. On this wall was a large mural of what the room behind this wall (not open to the public) looked like. It depicted a vast workroom filled with row after row of empty work stations for as far as the eye could see.

"I am always so struck by the power of the empty spaces at the mill. I think empty spaces are undervalued. They really tell you a lot. I come by this wall, this painting, every day giving tours, and it always makes me just stop, for a small moment or two, and think of who really filled that empty space. Its emptiness tells a lot. Thousands of workers came through this mill, many of them young, most of them women and majority of them immigrants. It looks empty now, but it is not. The people who worked here are long gone, but their stories stay forever and fill up these empty rooms. The rooms and the buildings here are gigantic. Huge. But these people, the workers, their stories make the place seem so small to me. I can feel it. To me it is real."

The Takeaway

I spent several hours at this museum. And while the work floors, the noisy machines, and the static exhibits were all excellent, it was the oral histories playing out of the monitors that have stayed with me ever since. Actually, that have haunted me ever since. I watched them all.

Each person, universally quite elderly, is identified by name and age. They speak a humble language, often in broken English. They describe the work at Boott as hard, proud, not for sissies.

The women tell of the indignities they suffered at the hands of male supervisors. The men share tales of backbreaking hard labor.

The one story that I will never forget is told by Narcissa Hodges, who worked on the factory room floor for forty-seven years. She says that all the young girls at the time had to wear hairnets for protection. One time a girl at the machine next to Narcissa took her hairnet off. A while later her long tresses got caught in one of the heavy, leather machine belts. The girl was pulled out of her chair by her hair. Narcissa and her fellow girl workers watched in horror as the girl died there, screaming, bleeding, and flailing from the top of the Weave Room ceiling. As Narcissa relates this story, she is obviously emotionally distressed.

I had tears coming down my face.

The Nuts and Bolts

Boott Cotton Mills Museum
115 John Street
Lowell, Massachusetts 01852
(978) 970-5000
http://www.nps.gov/lowe/planyourvisit/hours.htm
This museum is handicapped accessible.
Note: This museum is under the auspices of the National Park Service and is in fact a part of the Lowell National Historical Park.

Travel Suggestion

Parking can be difficult here. Much of the street parking is metered. A suggestion I found helpful (in the good weather) is to park at the National Historical Park Visitor's Center at 304 Dutton Street. Although this is several blocks away from the mill museum, you may leave your vehicle there all day and walk to the various museums in the historic district. Be sure and get your parking ticket validated at the center for free parking.

Museum Hours

November 29 through March 31: Monday to Friday, 12 p.m. to 4 p.m.; Saturday and Sunday, 12 p.m. to 5 p.m. April 1 through November 30: 9:30 a.m. to 5 p.m.

Admission

Adults: $6.00
Seniors (62+): $4.00
Children (6–16): $3.00
Students: $3.00

Up around the Bend

An entire afternoon can be crafted right here at the Boott Mill Museum. There is a "Mill Girls Exhibit" near the front of the complex. This is the last existing row of housing the mill girls would have stayed in. A small park is also at the entrance, with several interesting, large sculptures evoking the mill's past. Also there are canals and canal boat rides to explore. Several fine restaurants are just two blocks away in the center of Lowell.

REGION TWO

Greater Boston /Boston Metro

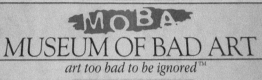

MUSEUM OF BAD ART

art too bad to be ignored™

DOWNSTAIRS

6 Museum of Bad Art

~~~

Somerville

This museum is in the most out of the way location of any in this book. But I encourage my readers to seek it out. It really is a sight to see.

The Museum of Bad Art (MOBA) is located in the remote basement of the old Somerville Theater cinema (you can see the water and heating pipes hanging from the ceiling). Buy a movie ticket and you get into MOBA free. If not, just email a request to info@MuseumofBadArt.org and a free ticket will be emailed to you.

"Believe it or not, we do have high standards," said Louise Reilly Sacco, the "Permanent Acting Interim Executive Director." "We are low tech for sure, but we do not accept any old piece of bad art to hang on our walls. We have over seven hundred pieces in our collection, and we rotate them so we can display about two dozen at one time here and more at our other locations."

The museum is a shrine to good intentions gone awry. Artists who got caught up in a frenzy of inspiration but failed to translate that to a work of art have found a gallery for themselves here in an old theater basement. It took me a while to actually "get" this museum, but once I did it was fun and very interesting. Sacco is proud of the selection on display and knows the minutiae of each painting. Most are bizarre, but all have a sort of macabre charm to them.

"My brother started this museum. He and a friend found an old painting in 1994 in the trash somewhere and took it for the frame. Someone's aunt had died, and they had thrown the portrait out. He decided to keep it. Soon he was scrounging roadside trash, flea markets, and junk sales for other pieces of bad art. When he accrued about fifty pieces, his collection evolved into the Museum of Bad Art. It was all tongue in cheek, of course, but people loved it. When a busload of seniors from Rhode Island showed up one day to see the paintings at his house, we knew we had to find a permanent home for the collection. And here it is," she said as she pointed to the room filled with, well, bad art.

"It's funny, but we take our mission very seriously. We have hundreds of items that people have brought to us or sent us. We get about a half-dozen submissions a week. We do examine each one, and most simply do not meet our 'bad art' standards."

I asked her what happens to these unwanted paintings. "Oh, we put them to good use," she replied. "Every few years we have a 'Rejection Collection Auction.' It is fun and we sell a lot of the paintings that night. Each piece comes with a certificate on the back which reads, 'This painting was *rejected* by the Museum of Bad Art.' People love it.

"We get visitors from all over the world. And the press recognition has been astounding. We have been featured in the *London Times, Rolling Stone* magazine, and others. We currently have thirty thousand people on our mailing list and more than forty thousand friends on Facebook. It really is amazing."

Amazing, yes. And bad. Very bad.

Wow Factor

Acknowledging that each painting was memorable, I asked Sacco which one was her wow factor, her favorite. She immediately walked me to the back of the small room, past a rolled up carpet remnant, and to a large oil painting facing against a back wall.

"I just love this guy," she said as she turned the painting around to show me. It is a large, elaborate acrylic painting inspired, no doubt, by the pointillist work of Georges Seurat. It is an odd portrait of, well, a man on a chamber pot. "There are just so many things about this painting that I love. It came to us untitled, but we named it *Sunday on the Pot with George.* The man, who is very overweight and appears to be staring intently into the distance, is sitting nearly naked on a pot. His flabby stomach strains against his white underpants. His hair is perfectly coiffed so as to suggest a toupee. His hands are on his knees. I try and put myself back to the day of the sitting for this painting. It is crafted quite professionally, employing the pointillism techniques we recognize. The shading is well done, and the colors show a smart nuance of technique. The man is surrounded by an elaborately designed bluish towel. Curiously, his naked legs extend to outside the frame. It is as if the artist lost interest in the painting. A man with no feet. But the artist definitely has talent. But why an overweight man in his tighty-whities. Who would ever pose for this? I love the mystery of this one."

Having seen all of the bad art on display here, I have to admit. This is one that will make even the casual viewer whisper under his or her breath, "wow."

The Takeaway

This museum is a pleasant surprise. Sure there are a lot of bad paintings on display, some horrendous. But with Sacco as your tour guide, you get a greater sense of what makes these significantly bad and at the same time so weirdly wonderful.

Here are some of her descriptions from my day at the museum. She obviously is partial to the paintings of famous people in the museum. She calls them "doppelhangers."

Marilyn Monroe: "This is clearly inspired by Philippe Halsman's dynamic *Jumpology* photograph. The photographer captured her famously posed in midair. This one is, well, not so famous. You can see that the painter got off to a good start, showing some talent in painting the star's face and capturing her ebullient personality. It really gets interesting when you get to her feet. So many artists have difficulty with the subject's feet. This one just gave up and gave Marilyn Monroe, one of the twentieth century's most beautiful women, what appears to be the feet of a very large man."

First Lady Mary Todd Lincoln: "A valiant effort. Mrs. Lincoln's large, gray face reminds one of the giant stone sculptures on Easter Island. This portrait was done on a lace tablecloth and is adorned with poinsettias. The First Lady appears to be wearing Hawaiian lei. It is wonderful."

Michael Jackson: "The singer just inspires people to paint. We have several portraits of him. This one is called *Man in the Mirror?* Michael's hair seems to be blown back by some sort of explosion.

And the configuration of him holding a microphone would be impossible for a human to replicate."

Donny and Marie Osmond: "This painting depicts the teenagers at the peak of their fame, around 1977. There is something strangely robotic about this depiction. And they have way too many teeth."

Joan Crawford: "This artist was obviously a fan of the Oscar-winning actress. But something went horribly wrong along the way. When asked, many people think this is a painting of wrestler Andre the Giant."

Elvis Presley: "The artist is Bonnie Daly, and she painted it in April of 1994. It has all the trappings of a Picasso work, weird stars floating erratically behind the singer. Elvis's image is out of proportion. He is dressed in a garish green jacket with a 'mobster' white tie. His famous pompadour looks top heavy as if to knock him down. But it is the pencil moustache that I like. So dashing, even though we cannot find that Elvis ever had a moustache. Bonnie named this *Pablo Presley*."

President John F. Kennedy: "The artist is unknown, and that is probably a good thing. The image shows our beloved president relaxing by eating an ice cream cone. Many agree with me. This painting is miraculous in that the artist has managed to turn one of our most handsome, photogenic leaders into a grotesque monster."

President Bill Clinton: "The artist gave it a good try. But what on earth is that below his chin. Is it a necktie or something maybe X-rated," she asked. (I looked. I blushed.)

Liza Minnelli: "This is all Liza," Sacco exclaimed. "The red lipstick, the sequined jacket, the theatrical eye makeup, the dangly earrings, the jazz hands. Perfect. Even right down to the chest hair!"

You get the idea.

The Nuts and Bolts

Museum of Bad Art

55 Davis Square (Somerville Theater)
Somerville, Massachusetts 02144
(781) 444-6757
www.museumofbadart.org
This museum is not handicapped accessible.

Note: There are two other Boston area MOBA locations.
Their addresses and information can be found at the
website.

Travel Suggestion

The Somerville Theater is the centerpiece of a busy,
trendy suburb of Boston. Its old-fashioned neon marquee
is a local landmark. You will find lots of interesting places
to eat and drink in Davis Square.

Museum Hours

As the MOBA website states, "Basically, we're open whenever films are running."

Admission

Free (with the purchase of a movie ticket)

Up around the Bend

Hey, this is Boston. The world awaits you around every corner!

7 The Sports Museum

Boston

TD Garden, one of the most hallowed sporting venues in the United States, is a place where good times are enjoyed, memories are made, and history calls at you from every corner. The original arena was torn down years ago, and this newer venue replaced it. Still, whether called the Boston Garden, the Fleet Center, TD Banknorth Garden, or any other name, it is known for all immortality as just "The Garden," for this is the place where championships are too many to count, iconic moments are frozen in time, and the ghosts of our youth come alive. Whether on the boards, on ice, or in the stands, the Garden is nothing less than a shrine to those in Boston. Some say if you sniff your nose in certain places, you can still smell the smoke coming out of one of Red Auerbach's famous Cohiba Limited Edition Double Corona cigars.

BOSTON, USA—SEP 29, 2017: Statue the goal of famous sportsman Bobby Orr by travelview/Shutterstock.

"Ah, the cigar. Yes, Red was the only person allowed by Boston city fire marshals to smoke inside the new building," Brian Codagnone told me.

And to many, Brian Codagnone has the best job in the world.

"Yes, I am very lucky," Codagnone told me recently during a tour of the Sports Museum inside the Garden. He is the associate curator of the museum, which was formerly known as the Sports Museum of New England. It contains dozens of colorful vintage sports uniforms, hundreds of artifacts from every imaginable sport (heavy on the Boston area), and too many heart-in-your-throat action photographs to even count. The exhibit space is spread out over two floors around the perimeter of the premium seating area.

"The museum originally opened in Brighton in 1977, and I started there as a volunteer the very next year. I've been associated with it ever since. We highlight all of the New England professional sports teams, both past and present, as well as sporting events such as the Boston Marathon and the Olympics, here in several floors of exhibit space. We call the arena itself our biggest exhibit. People love to see the banners and the floor, whether it be parquet or ice, depending on what is going on that day. A lot of times, for example, Celtics fans will go on the tour and say, 'Hey, how come there is so much black and gold in here (the colors of the NHL Boston Bruins hockey team)?' I have to tell them it is because the Bruins own the building. The Celtics don't even practice here, and they have their own basketball offices across the street," he said as he pointed to a brick building right outside one of the large windows that encase the building. And, by the way, this is a view that also showcases the Bunker Hill Monument, the masts of the tall ships in Boston Harbor including Old Ironsides, as well as the iconic Zakim Bridge.

"History is all around us," the curator commented. "And, inside here too."

The museum is an experience in sensory overload for the sports fanatic. Clearly the Bruins and the Celtics get top billing, but the Boston Red Sox and New England Patriots are close behind. Other featured sections include those dedicated to New England college football, the Atlanta Braves (which started here), the Boston Marathon, women's sports history (including an exhibit on Title IX), and others. "This is really a living museum," Codagnone said. "Many of these great legends that you see highlighted here still live in the Boston area and visit us. We have several generations of fans who come here. I enjoy it when grandfathers bring in their little kids and start telling them their stories of the past. It is great. There are just so many memories in here."

I asked the curator what was the biggest attraction at this museum beyond the Garden itself. "That is easy. The parquet floor," he said with a smile. "It's the most famous floor in basketball history. They get reflective and almost reverential. The first thing some people say when they get here is, 'I want to see the floor.' I will never forget the time we had someone here who took out his cell phone and took a video of himself in the arena and was sending it to his father in the Ukraine," he laughed.

As we walked around the floors of the museum, the names and faces that stared out at me are a virtual hall of fame of sports heroes. Ted Williams, Doc Rivers, Larry Bird, Bill Russell, Doug Flutie, Carl Yastrzemski, Bobby Orr, and so many others. If Cooperstown has a contender for best sports hall of fame, it has to be this place right here along the river in downtown Boston.

This museum is sports "bucket list" material.

Wow Factor

"Oh, that is easy," Brian Codagnone said. "Let me show you the sculptures."

On Level 9 of the Garden is an array of life-sized sports sculptures so realistic they will make you look twice. "Armand LaMontagne is a sculptor of world renown. He is from Rhode Island. His statues can be found all over, and his most famous one is probably the Babe Ruth statue which greets visitors to the National Baseball Hall of Fame in Cooperstown. He created this series of amazing sculptures, and to me these are about as close to being with these personalities as you can get."

The collection includes hockey legend Bobby Orr, basketball star Larry Bird, sluggers Ted Williams and Carl Yastrzemski, and others. "The detail of each sculpture is unbelievable. If you notice, the pinkie finger on Larry Bird's right hand is deformed as it is in real life. And look at this basketball in his hands," he said. I examined it closely. The realism was fantastic. "Armand tells me there are 50,000 dimples in that one ball alone. I'll take his word for it!"

One thing that struck me was the Ted Williams pose. "LaMontagne always liked portraying Ted. He was a favorite of the artist. So he wanted to do a little something different for this one." Different? I guess so. The sculpture shows Williams salmon fishing, a passion the ball player enjoyed for decades. The image, carved out of a 1,600-pound chunk of laminated basswood, shows the towering Williams in wool shirt, high-waisted waders, and rubber boots, holding a fishing rod in one hand and a sizable Atlantic salmon in the other. He sports the classic 1950s-style haircut that he wore until the end of his life. Williams enjoyed all of the sculptor's wooden images of him but said this "fishing" one was his favorite. *Life* magazine reported that when the Splendid Splinter attended the unveiling of his wooden statue at the National Baseball Hall of Fame in Cooperstown, he wept. The magazine called the article "A Legendary Hitter Chokes."

"I am always walking these halls, rearranging items, and straightening things that get off kilter when the building shakes. We are a working arena, after all. I also give tours, etc. But I always pause when I get to the sculptures."

The Takeaway

If you are a sports fan, especially a fan of Boston area teams, you have found nirvana here. But even if you are not a fan, there will be plenty of eye-candy for you to enjoy. The photographs alone, some of the most exciting, iconic pictures ever taken in the world of sports, are all here for you to enjoy.

The purpose of this book is to tease the reader to go and visit these museums. To give you just enough information to wet your whistle, if you will. That is hard to do with the Sports Museum. There are just so many indelible, unforgettable items here that I just have to share a few of them with you.

Adam Vinatieri's shoes are here. Yes, his shoes. Who could forget his immortal "Snow Kick" in the 2001 AFC Division Playoff between the Patriots and the Oakland Raiders, a kick that ESPN has called the greatest moment in the franchise history? Vinatieri sealed the win for the New England Patriots with a soaring, forty-five-yard launch, in blizzard whiteout conditions, while wearing two different shoes. One was a football shoe, the other a soccer shoe. Both are here.

Doug Flutie's "Hail Mary Pass" game jersey is also here, recalling that dramatic moment on November 23, 1984, when quarterback

Flutie hurled the pigskin more than sixty yards into the Velcro hands of Gerard Phelan in the end zone for the Boston College win over the Miami Hurricanes, 47–45. The clock showed no time left in the game when he threw the pass.

With a nod to this being a museum for all New England area sports, one of the most unusual items here is Manute Bol's basketball warmup suit. Many forget that Bol, who came from Sudan, played for the University of Bridgeport in Connecticut before going on to the NBA. Bol's warmup suit is hard to miss. It covers more than two whole sections of a large exhibit case. Bol was tied with Gheorghe Muresan as the tallest player ever to don an NBA jersey. He stood seven feet seven inches tall.

Perhaps the most beloved figure in all of New England sports is slugger Ted Williams. There are many of Ted's artifacts, newspaper articles, photographs, paintings (also by LaMontagne), and memorabilia in this museum. Perhaps the centerpiece is the legend's actual locker from the Red Sox locker room. It is exactly as it was on the hitter's last day at Fenway and still carries his name on it. The inside of the locker, now a shrine for Red Sox Nation and baseball fans everywhere, can be viewed through a glass covering. It contains many Ted Williams–era artifacts.

Possibly the saddest, most emotional item here is "The Ball That Changed History." It's the baseball that hit Red Sox player Tony Conigliaro in the eye in 1967, essentially ending his career. Brian Codagnone, the curator who accompanied me throughout my tour, lowered his voice when he described the impact of this baseball: "Tony C. was a very popular ball player in Boston. He was a hometown guy. Everybody loved him. He had a lot of spirit, and made a great comeback after his devastating injury. After he got hit, baseball changed the rules and made the side ear-flap a standard part of the batting helmet. Too bad. We loved him. He died when he was only forty-five years old."

This museum is filled with stories like that. Stirring, poignant, emotional stories. Stories with heart.

The Nuts and Bolts

The Sports Museum

TD Garden
100 Legends Way
Boston, Massachusetts 02114
(617) 624-1234
www.sportsmuseum.org
This museum is handicapped accessible.

Travel Suggestion

The museum is located inside the TD Garden, which is located on the edge of busy downtown Boston. It is near the famous North End neighborhood, which is popular for all of its Italian restaurants and food stores. The North End is also the oldest of Boston's many walkable neighborhoods.

Museum Hours

Tickets may be purchased at the Level 2 Pro Shop, and this is where tours begin, on the hour every day. The last tour begins at 3 p.m. The museum encompasses Levels 5 and 6 of the arena.
Monday through Friday, 10 a.m. to 4 p.m.;
Saturday and Sunday, 11 a.m. to 4 p.m.

Note: The museum is closed on days when there are games, events, conventions, etc. Be sure and check the website before your visit.

Admission

Adults: $12.00
Students (10–18) and seniors (65+): $10.00
Children under 10: Free

Up around the Bend

A world of history, culture, excitement, fine dining, and fun are all at your doorstep after you leave this museum. The famous Quincy Market, the Freedom Trail, Old Ironsides, Bunker Hill, and many other Boston landmarks are all within a mile of this museum.

8 Boston Tea Party Ships and Museum

Boston

"We get visitors from all over the country as well as from all over the world. You should see the look on the faces of the visitors coming through here from Great Britain," said Shawn Ford, vice president and executive director of this museum. "They have a much different reaction to the story of the colonists' rebellion against their king than we do."

The Boston Tea Party Ships and Museum is a comprehensive, multilevel, and highly entertaining stage on which one of America's greatest stories plays out. "I am so proud of our actors," Ford said. "They enjoy their work here, they really invest themselves in the characters and roles they play, and they are the ones who really should get credit for making this such a fun place to discover an important chapter in American history."

The actors, dressed in period costumes and employing their best British accents, welcome visitors at the get-go and stay with the group throughout a one-hour tour, both on land and on water. On the tour your experience begins in a replica of an old Boston meetinghouse. It is December 16, 1773, late afternoon. Prominent local leaders are trying to rally the citizenry to stand up against the king's tea tax. Each visitor is given an ID card upon entering. I took the tour, and mine described me as "Joshua Wyeth, a blacksmith and one of only two residents who came this night from Cambridge." My card went on to say that "I was fully aware of the severity of tonight's actions and will carry its importance with me for the rest of my life."

An actor portraying Samuel Adams leads the assembled crowd (the tourists) in a rousing, foot-stomping, huzzah-shouting, fie-cursing revolt that eventually spills out of the building, down Griffin's Wharf, and on to the *Eleanor* afloat on the water.

The *Eleanor* is a magnificent recreation of one of the actual ships that brought the tea into the harbor that fateful night. We, the rebellious visitors, clamor aboard the ship and assemble in the center. Our docent, dressed in long stockings, vest, and tri-cornered hat, dramatically explains what is in store for us this evening. Death by hanging will certainly be our sentence if we are caught. Still we carry on. "Huzzah!" On the deck, alongside the ship's railing, we find large crates of tea. "Dump the tea!" is the cry, and several volunteers from our group step forward and actually throw these parcels into the harbor. It is all very exhilarating.

"That is our favorite part," Ford said. "As you could see, our staff usually picks out the younger visitors to come forward and actually throw the (tethered) tea chests into the water. They do it with great gusto. I am certain it is something these kids will never forget doing. And that is what makes our museum so charming. It is hands-on all the way."

After a brief tour of the *Eleanor* we are escorted into the museum where we enter a dimly lit room. A tea chest twirls slowly on a backlit pedestal. It is an original from the revolt. A wide variety of large oil portraits line the room. At one point during the presentation the oil paintings come to life. King George III and patriot leader Sam Adams shout and argue vociferously at each other, constrained only by their gilt-edged picture frames. It is quirky, startling, and surprisingly effective. Every line the "portrait actors" recite is taken from actual letters exchanged by revolutionary protagonists.

From this room we enter a small theater. Once seated, the curtains part and we view an eleven-minute, award-winning film, *Let It Begin Here,* which deals with the events after the Tea Party and up to the battles at Lexington and Concord on April 19, 1775, the day of the firing of "the shot heard 'round the world." This is a dramatic and beautifully filmed narrative of the events. The acting is superb, the sets are realistic, and the story is gripping. Adding to the top-notch quality of this final tour stop is the fact that this is a *four*-dimensional film. With every musket blast a hidden air cannon spits out a jet of air onto the audience. "Butt kickers" jostle the floor under our feet, keeping time with the thundering horses on the screen.

I was sincerely impressed by the whole production.

Wow Factor

"We have so many wow factors here," Ford began. "We built our ships to exact specifications to make them as similar to the ships of the time as possible. On the *Eleanor* alone we used over 22,000 hand-driven nails. We also used copper that came from the Revere Copper Products Company in upstate New York. That, by its very nature, brings the history back here to Revere's Old Boston."

"Still it is hard to beat the tea chest," he smiled. "That one little box twirling around in the glass case in the museum is our holy grail. It is an actual tea chest that was dumped overboard by the patriots back in 1773."

So, how did the tea chest resurface after all of these years?

"Interesting. A fifteen-year-old boy named John Robinson found it floating in the water along a South Boston beach right after the Tea Party. He took it home and hid it. It was in his family from then until we got it. What happened was that we received a phone call one day from a family in Laredo, Texas, and they told us they had an original Boston Tea Party tea chest in their home. It was in their living room. Over the years the young members of their family used it to store dolls in. Well, that sounded pretty curious so we went down and looked at it. It seemed convincing so we had it examined. Scientists and archivists did all sorts of tests, ultimately proving that it was the real thing.

"They saw that the tea stains on the inside of the chest could only have come from English tea of that era. The metal lid clasps were the same as those used in the 1700s. The salt water residue in the wood was the same as that of the water in Boston Harbor. The screws. The type of wood. The paint. It all checked out.

"We couldn't believe it. It is one of only two original Boston Tea Party tea chests in existence. One is at the D.A.R. [Daughters of the American Revolution] Headquarters in Washington, D.C. And the other is right here. Incredible."

I asked the director how it feels having that iconic artifact from America's beginnings here in the museum.

"You know, it is very hard to own something from an event. Over 240 years ago that crate was thrown overboard in a courageous act of defiance. It was dumped into this very body of water, a young boy found it, and eventually it came home. It is fitting that it be showcased here at a museum of the most important event leading to our freedom. I like to say that there is a magical 'man behind the curtain' quality to our museum. And having that original tea chest here for all to see is just a wonderful, extra-special treat for us and for the country as well."

The Takeaway

This is one of Boston's great museums. It is a little hard to get to, situated in the middle of a bridge in the busy downtown area, and parking can be problematic. Still, having been to dozens of museums similar to this one, I have to say this is done spectacularly. Younger visitors, perhaps fifteen and under, will gain much from visiting here, and there is never a dull moment. Adults will enjoy the narrative, the acting, and the high quality of the presentations.

The Nuts and Bolts

Boston Tea Party Ships and Museum
306 Congress Street
Boston, Massachusetts 02210
(866) 955-0667
https://bostonteapartyship.com
This museum is handicapped accessible. However, wheelchairs are not allowed into the hold of the *Eleanor* because of the cramped quarters. Costumed docents will stay above and give those who cannot go below a description of what can be seen down in the ship.

Travel Suggestion

As stated earlier, this museum is located halfway across the downtown Congress Street Bridge. Because of this parking will be about a five-minute walk or so from either end of the bridge. There are several lots to choose from, and parking tickets can be validated for a discount by the museum.

Museum Hours

Hour-long tours begin at 10 a.m. and end at 5 p.m. daily.

Admission

Adults: $28.00
Seniors and students: $25.00
Children (5–12): $18.00
Discounts are available by purchasing tickets in advance on the website.

Up around the Bend

Located just two blocks away from the Boston Tea Party Museum on the same street is the Boston Fire Museum. This is a small museum located in a historically significant 1891 firehouse. Many old fire trucks, fire apparatus, and displays are located inside the giant engine doors. The building is architecturally significant and constructed out of stone and red brick. Notice there are no support poles holding up the main floor ceiling, no columns at all. That is because it's held up by trusses from above. For more information, see http://www.bostonfiremuseum.com.

9 Museum of the National Center of Afro-American Artists

Boston

"The fact that this museum even exists today is a miracle," said Edmund Barry Gaither. He is the director and curator of the Museum of the National Center of Afro-American Artists. "It was quite a journey. Quite a journey."

I met with Gaither in his cluttered office in the basement of the museum. He told me of the dream that started it all.

"That dream would belong to one Elma Lewis. She was a powerful, pioneering force behind this museum from the beginning. Ms. Lewis grew up in the Roxbury neighborhood of Boston and always dreamed of having a place here where African American youth could gather and hone their artistic talents. Roxbury is the

physical center of the city of Boston, the heart of the city. Lewis was a brilliant woman who was in fact among the first group of nationally recognized MacArthur Fellowship Grants, known as the 'Genius Prize.' Others that first year included poet Robert Penn Warren, writer Cormac McCarthy, and playwright Derek Wolcott.

"The concept that Ms. Lewis put forth was to provide the greatest support of great ideas that were small enough so that there would not be a lot of infighting. She started with dance in the 1960s when there was a great new consciousness among black youth and where opportunities were limited in her community. But she persevered and brought many artistic performers to the Roxbury neighborhood. One of her great friends, composer Duke Ellington, would come here frequently and give performances. He would stay overnight at Ms. Lewis's own modest home. By the late 1960s, she had many students and focused on a permanent home for her school. She had a simple business strategy: we need a school to teach dance, we need a theater to teach performing arts, we need ensemble space for music students, and we want a museum for those talented in the visual arts. That museum is where we are sitting today," Gaither told me.

"Over the years she created important, strong bonds with other institutions such as the New England Conservatory of Music and the Museum of Fine Arts. In 1969, I was teaching at Spelman College in Atlanta when she called me and asked me to join her 'big, bold endeavor.' She had a great knack for finding people, good people, who were attracted to the largeness of her ideas. She did not want a storefront museum; she wanted it to have a small yet robust presence in the community with five important pillars: its exhibitions, that it hold its own collection, that it would create research material, that it held public programs, and that we publish. We have done all of that."

The museum is housed in a grand old mansion built in 1872 for a wealthy Boston industrialist. "Here is the miracle part," Gaither said. "We finally acquired this building, then known as Abbotsford, in 1970. It was owned by the school next door, and it was scheduled for demolition. Boston mayor Kevin White stepped in and the city took it over. It sat disintegrating for a time. Soon the city was rocked by racial violence. The busing issue was the hot topic of the day, and it was just such an uncertain time. The mayor, probably for political reasons, let this building go. And that is when we stepped in and took over. It was a shock when we did our first tour of the mansion.

"The building had been raped. The copper thieves had stripped the place, the iron heat radiators had been scrapped, the lights were missing, even the slate roof tiles were gone. It was ruined. But, as I always say, a miracle happened. I had already scheduled our first major show for the still-unfinished museum. The American Association of Museums was meeting in Boston, and I had convinced them to come and visit our venue. We had very little to show them, but I knew this would be our big moment to shine. The mansion was virtually empty, but with the help of an army of volunteers and a lot of hard work we did it. Just before the opening of the exhibit for the association, I went to a salvage yard and found two old Gothic-looking church chandeliers. I told the owner that I needed them but had no money. He was gracious enough to give them to me and to allow me to pay later. So we installed them. Before the big crowd of conventioneers arrived, I went out and bought large sheets of blue paper and covered the floors with them because I did not even have carpeting. The next thing I knew, a parade of buses came pulling up with about seven hundred museum experts in them. They came through our new mansion home, walking on the blue paper and everything, and loved it. Our debut had a full house. It was a great success. Of course, I have no idea how we did that. But we did, and we are still here," he laughed.

Wow Factor

"We have many wonderful pieces on our collection. So many bright new African American artists. Just beautiful. But unfortunately, I cannot show you the wow factor because it is packed up and ready to go on loan. But let me tell you about it. It is a famous painting by the artist Charles White. It is titled *Nat Turner: Yesterday. Today. Tomorrow.* It is an epic piece, and in fact was the very first item ever given to this museum. We could never have afforded it, but it was donated to us by the Boston Black United Front, an early civil rights group in our city. Someone from that group saw it in Charles White's gallery in Los Angeles, bought it, and gave it to us. I always say that this work was a commission for us. It was a promise for our future, ensuring that we would have a wonderful museum to house this wondrous piece of art and other great works. The piece is so bold, so inspirational. Many African American politicians have asked us to loan it to them during their time in office, from the Supreme Court and to the governor's office. We are very careful about who we loan this to. It is our most in-demand loan item. It stands almost five feet tall and shows Nat Turner swooning and surrendering himself so that he will reenergize his strive. An agitated bird flutters over all. Nat's face is in apotheosis, becoming almost as if a divine spirit. It reflects the turbulence of his life. It is a masterpiece and has been in every major Charles White retrospective across the country. We just packed it up to send it out so I cannot show you it. But, yes, that is clearly my own, and this museum's, wow factor."

The Takeaway

I found several important takeaways from this museum. The fact that it exists at all (Gaither's "miracle story") is just one of them. On the day of my visit there were several exciting exhibits on display in a half-dozen rooms by artists such as Dan Jay, Stephen Hamilton, and Johnetta Tinker. A large gathering of the public was going on in a conference area, and a docent was leading around a small group of women. Outside the large arched open doorways I could hear the squeal of neighborhood children at play on a sunny autumn afternoon. The mansion sits high on a hill as if lording over its host neighborhood. It has a regal presence. The most intriguing piece of all (to me) sits on the front lawn of the museum. Titled *Eternal Presence,* the sculpture by John Wilson is that of an African American male head sitting on the lawn. The sculpture stops at the man's shoulders. It is a magnificent piece created in 1987. The head is seven feet tall and appears to be keeping watch over the children playing nearby. It perfectly captures the essence of this museum.

The Nuts and Bolts

**Museum of the National Center
of Afro-American Artists**
300 Walnut Avenue
Boston, Massachusetts 02119
(617) 442-8614
www.ncaaa.org
This museum is handicapped accessible.

Travel Suggestion

This museum is a little tricky to find as it is located in a crowded neighborhood with small, winding roads. GPS would be the best tool to use if you are driving as there are few signs leading you to the museum. To use public transportation: from Ruggles Station on the Orange Line, or Dudley Station, take bus no. 22 (Ashmont Station/Ruggles Station) to Walnut Avenue at Seaver Street. Walk along Walnut Avenue—away from Franklin Park—for three blocks. The museum entrance gate is in the third block just beyond the David A. Ellis School. The 22 bus runs approximately every fifteen minutes.

Museum Hours

Tuesday through Sunday, 1 p.m. to 5 p.m.

Admission

Adults: $5.00
Seniors and children: $4.00
Phone ahead for large group tour information.

Up around the Bend

There are several historic buildings in the Roxbury neighborhood of Boston. One of the best is the Shirley-Eustis House, 33 Shirley Street. This is the home of royal governor William Shirley (1741–49) and is the only remaining "country house" built by a British royal governor. Tours are offered; see www.shirleyeustishouse.org.

Photo courtesy of Metropolitan Waterworks Museum.

10 Waterworks Museum

Boston

If there is a museum that is a monument to industrial beauty, this is it.

"Yes, it is magnificent isn't it?" Eric Metzger said proudly.

He was the director of museum services at the Waterworks Museum on the day of my visit. The "it" he was referring to was a massive display of engineering history splayed out on the floor far below us. We were standing in the Overlook Gallery, two stories high, gazing down at the Great Engines Hall, which contains several behemoth pumping mechanisms; a dazzling chorus line of historic steam engines; a labyrinth of walkways, staircases, and passageways; and a veritable history of the water supply system, from its inception, for the entire city of Boston.

"We believe that our collection of the three massive pumping engines you see in front of us makes us a unique destination, perhaps in the world. As the city grew, its need for water grew with it, and the Chestnut Hill Pumping Station was constructed to help meet that need. The Chestnut Hill Reservoir, which is directly across the street from the museum, was the ultimate water supply, which ran through this station and ultimately on to millions of Bostonians and metropolitan area residents. These huge engines pumped the water through thousands of miles of underground pipes to locations throughout the burgeoning area."

One does not need to know much about the inner workings of the complex pumping apparatus on display here. They are eye-popping industrial architectural marvels in and of themselves. Take the Leavitt engine, the largest of the three.

"This pumping engine is certainly unique in that it not only was an engineering wonder when it was built, but also for the fact that it was constructed with an eye for beauty. I know that sounds odd but look at this machine," Metzger pointed out. "Its size is overwhelming, towering two stories above the floor, but look how graceful it also is. This was by design."

When entering the museum floor, the sheer size of the Leavitt engine makes it almost impossible to fully take in the heft of the machine. But from the second floor viewing gallery, one can easily see that this was designed to be efficient and also appealing to look at. Graceful, curved work decks accentuate the brass and copper railings, cast-iron fittings and compartments, and steel plating. "Erasmus Leavitt, Jr., was the premier designer of custom water pumps of his era. And he wanted these workhorses to also be pleasing to the eye. For example, look at this touch over there," Metzger said pointing to the top of the engine in front of us.

Here one can plainly see large sections of the engine, which beautifully contrasted with the heavy industrial usage planned for it. "That is shiny, black walnut hardwood," he said. "On a water pumping engine. Amazing. That is a perfect example of how Mr. Leavitt designed his machines. He wanted them to perform precisely, of course, but he wanted them to be aesthetically pleasing as well. He wanted them to be classy, showy, and evocative of the grandeur of Old Boston. In 1895, after this engine went fully operational, *Scientific American* magazine sent reporters here to witness this incredible machine for themselves."

There are two other massive pumping engines on the museum floor: the Worthington, which was built in Buffalo, and the Allis, which was built in Milwaukee. The Leavitt was made in Boston.

"All three pumps were shipped to this station by train, piece by piece." Metzger walked me to the back of the building and showed me the original tall doors that would be swung open to allow access to the railroad tracks directly behind the building. "From here the workers would muscle the heavy pieces inside using block and tackle devices. This was the era when things are built by hand."

The museum building is stunning. Built in the Richardson-Romanesque style, the architect was Arthur Vinal. He was one of New England's most prolific municipal architects and in fact was the city architect of Boston from 1884 to 1887. This massively elegant High Service Pumping Station here at Chestnut Hill is considered one of his crowning achievements.

"This was a major landmark in this area for generations of Bostonians. The Chestnut Hill Reservoir was one of the most popular gathering places for locals back in the day. Men in suits would drive women in their fancy dresses out here in horse carriages where they would enjoy a day in the country around the reservoir. In fact a driveway (carriage path), which encircles the body of water, was constructed for that very purpose. The reservoir and the driveway contributed to what eventually is considered the Golden Age of Boston in the second half of the nineteenth century," he said.

The museum grounds, the complex of historic buildings, and the recreational allure of the reservoir still make this a popular place. On the day I visited the Waterworks Museum the area was buzzing with runners, bikers, dog-walkers, and pleasure seekers all enjoying the bucolic atmosphere. And a lot of them were young people.

"Yes, the young people love it out here. Of course, with thirteen thousand Boston College students located right next door to us that is expected," he noted.

Wow Factor

The wow factor for Metzger was an easy one.

"Without a doubt, the three engines. They are just so histori-cally and aesthetically interesting. Most people have never seen anything like them. Large steam engines such as these were vital to the development of Boston. In the 1800s, the city had a decision to make. They needed water desperately. They could either take it from the closest location, the polluted rivers adjacent to the urban area, or they could take it from reservoirs that would be constructed in less-populated rural areas. They chose the latter. In doing so, Boston developed a plan for watershed conservation that was considered a model for the nation, including the construction of the Quabbin Reservoir of western Massachusetts. And along the way they gave its citizens some of the sweetest, unfiltered water of any urban area. In fact, even today our water consistently ranks among the top three large urban systems in the United States.

"I am an archeologist by profession, so for me there are many levels of attraction to the history represented by the Waterworks Museum. The engines and engineering aspect are of course the forefront. The social history in this museum's lineage takes it directly back to the glory days of the founding of Boston. The architecture has a historic prominence in its own right, too. Vinal was very meticulous and proud of his monumental creation at Chestnut Hill. In fact, he even carved little images of his and his wife's faces near the top of the tower of the pumping station. And finally, the public health aspect of what they did here was significant for the future of Massachusetts. Building the infrastructure for the delivery of clean, safe, and healthy drinking water to a city the size of Boston is just an astounding chapter in the history of Massachusetts that is aptly conveyed by the Waterworks Museum history.

"This place is the epicenter of so many incredible Boston stories."

The Takeaway

This museum is truly one of Boston's great secrets. The tours, conducted by museum staff members, are fascinating. What I enjoyed most was that as we walked the pump station floor, absorbing the minutiae of the science of these gigantic pumping monsters, you really are surrounded by the incredible beauty, of bricks, stone, cast-iron, and steel brought together for form and function. Arches swoop over there, tall windows let light in over here, the two- and three-story engines loom above all like old passenger ships emerging from a morning darkness, their lights twinkling and their brass railings gleaming, and the exterior of the building is shrouded in Victorian-era fancywork.

I guess it is hard really to describe this marriage of industrial usefulness and such mechanical beauty. As a testament to this theory, however, let me offer this.

On the day I visited the Waterworks Museum. I saw something very unusual for a place of this type. Scattered throughout the vast museum floor, in corners, in the shadow of the lumbering Leavitt engine, in the back near the old wooden railroad doors were scores of art students. They were hard at work drawing and painting what I find so hard to describe in words.

The remarkable beauty of this surprising place.

The Nuts and Bolts

Waterworks Museum

2450 Beacon Street
Boston, Massachusetts 02467
(617) 277-0065
http://waterworksmuseum.org
This museum is handicapped accessible.

Travel Suggestion

The museum is located five miles west of the center city area of Boston. It is easily accessible from the MBTA Green C or D Lines. Driving, follow Beacon Street to the Chestnut Hill Reservoir area. Parking is available.

Museum Hours

November 1 through March 31: Wednesday to Sunday, 11 a.m. to 4 p.m.
April 1 through October 31: Wednesday, 11 a.m. to 9 p.m. Thursday to Sunday, 11 a.m. to 4 p.m.

Admission

Free

Up around the Bend

No visit to this museum would be complete without a stroll around the Chestnut Hill Reservoir. It is a leisurely 1.5-mile walk and offers a splendid viewpoint of the reservoir, the Waterworks Museum complex, some old original gatehouses, and sections of the campus of Boston College. The reservoir has been listed on the National Register of Historic Places and has been designated a City of Boston Landmark. Also, the Quabbin Reservoir is located an hour and a half west of Boston. A visit here will show you the magnitude of the creation of the water system for the city of Boston and much of eastern Massachusetts. The reservoir is the largest body of water in Massachusetts, and four towns were evacuated for its building: Dana, Enfield, Greenwich, and Prescott.

Photograph by Biruitorul. Available at: https://commons.wikimedia.org/wiki/
File:LarzAAutoM.JPG.

Larz Anderson
Auto
Museum

Brookline

In 1899, Larz Anderson wed Isabel Weld Perkins. Anderson was by then a seasoned U.S. diplomat who had already served his country around the world and who would go on to serve in the diplomatic corps for many more years including a stint as U.S. ambassador to Japan. Perkins came from one of New England's wealthiest and most prominent families. Her father, Commodore George Perkins, was a Civil War hero who captained the USS *Cayuga* with distinction. Her grandfather on the other side of the family, William Fletcher Weld, was one of the most successful shipping magnates of his time. When Grandfather Weld died in 1881, his fortune rolled down through the family ranks. Isabel's inheritance from him totaled more than $3 million. This made her one of the wealthiest females in America.

She was five years old.

The marriage of Larz and Isabel was the catalyst of one of the great love stories in the history of American high society. The two entertained lavishly, bequeathed magnanimously, served their fellow man fervently, and enjoyed a wanderlust that led them to the far corners of the earth. Literally. In fact, they are reported to have been among the very first Westerners to set foot in Tibet.

And they collected automobiles. Lots of them.

"The Larz Anderson Auto Museum is America's oldest car collection," Sheldon Steele, executive director of the museum, told me. "The Andersons began collecting cars after first seeing an automobile on the streets of Paris during a visit there. They made their first purchase that year, an 1899 Winton. That would be the beginning of a long relationship between the couple and their collection. They purchased a new car every year from 1899 to 1948. The Andersons would use the vehicle and then often after a year 'retire' it to the carriage house on their grounds. We have those vehicles here on display for the public, including that very first car, the 1899 Winton."

The carriage house of which Steele spoke is a large, chateau-like structure built on the grounds of the Anderson estate. Their residence here, "Weld," a sprawling, twenty-five-room mansion that provided a long, sweeping view of the city of Boston, was torn down in 1955. In fact, the carriage house was inspired and designed after the famous Chateau Chaumont in the Loire Valley of France. The carriage house is now home of the Larz Anderson Auto Museum.

And it is magnificent.

"This grand area of the main exhibit room was used for the Anderson's horses and vehicles. Each of their prized horses had their own stable with all the then-modern conveniences at hand,"

Steele told me as we walked the pristine showroom floor. Each stable is roomy and airy. The floor has a slanted, herringbone brick pattern with a large grooming drain in the center. Overhead are large, roll-top overhead doors that when pulled down create a substantial walled-in space in the center. Along the walls of the back stable are the names of the Anderson's prized horses. There are grooming areas, a place for horses to receive medical attention or to give birth, feeding stations, and more. It was clearly state of the art for its era.

"There was even an innovative method for collecting the horse's manure. It was gathered and taken from the building where it was transported to the top of the property. There the manure was spread among the many elaborate greenhouses to fertilize the prized flowers and landscape plantings used on the estate."

A separate tack room holds a dazzling display of saddles and equine accoutrements. Each saddle bears a silver Anderson-family crest. A display case of contest ribbons attests to the quality of the horses that came from "Weld."

"Mrs. Anderson had some of the finest horses in New England, and she stabled them here," Director Steele told me. "She was an excellent equestrian and was a free-spirited woman. She was known to drive her magnificent team of horses through the city streets of Boston. Mrs. Anderson was also the first woman in Massachusetts to hold a driver's license."

The main floor of the fifteen-thousand-square-foot cathedral-like carriage house is used for a series of rotating displays. The Andersons' car collection is on the lower level.

"The Andersons were eager collectors. Here, we see the results of this. All of the cars here are in original condition, and all of them were used personally by the Andersons," Steele told me.

The collection is a veritable encyclopedia of early international automobile designs. A 1926 Lincoln is an example of one of the first limousines. You couldn't miss the 1912 Renault coming down the road. It sports no less than eight brass horns to make its presence known. And, yes, the little 1899 Winton is here too. It is a small, plain, one-cylinder buggy that shrinks in comparison to the larger, more ornate cars of the latter part of the collection.

"This is really a remarkable vehicle," Steele said as we approached one of the largest. "It is a 1906 Charron-Girodot-Voight. It was the Anderson's traveling car. It had all of the modern amenities one could imagine. It cost $23,000 to have it designed. And contained folding beds, a communication device for the passenger to speak to the driver, a library, a heating unit, a wash basin, and a porcelain commode."

I suggested to the director that this vehicle, with all the comforts of home, must have been Mrs. Anderson's favorite car in the collection.

"No, she really liked this one the most," he said as he walked me to a 1908 Bailey Electric Phaeton Victoria. "In the day, women were expected to wear flowing dresses, long scarves, big unwieldy bonnets, and such. With a regular automobile you can imagine how dirty their clothes would become. Not so with this electric car. It was clean, had easy maneuverability, and was very quiet. Mrs. Anderson used this as her personal vehicle for twenty years."

Wow Factor

Despite all of the automobile history on display at this museum, Steele's wow factor was a curious piece of furniture.

"In the early part of the twentieth century, Boston was known for their huge, grandiose automobile dealerships. These were really the great business salons of the era. They were basically auto palaces. One of the largest and most famous 'temples of the wheel' was the H. K. Noyes Buick dealer at 855 Commonwealth Avenue. In

February of 1921, the Buick Company gifted the Noyes dealership with what is known as the Noyes Bench."

The bench is unlike anything I have ever seen. Made out of English lime wood, this large piece of furniture (yes, it is actually a bench for the showroom) features a series of carvings depicting the history of transportation. The right side of the frieze shows the "Eastern World" and begins by depicting workers laboriously hauling products on their backs, the construction of the pyramids, and the carrying of parcels on a variety of beasts of burden like camels and horses. The left side of the bench depicts the "Western World" and shows a lead-up in transportation advances from peddle carts to rickshaws to early automobiles to trains, boats, and modern trucks.

Above all, in the carved sky, are the latest in aviation transportation options available at the time, including dirigibles and biplanes. In the center is a tall, Big Ben–like clock made by the Waltham Watch Company. At the top of each hour it would chime out three melodies. The Noyes Bench was carved by Ernesto Pellegrini, one of Boston's top furniture makers. A plaque in the center reads: "Presented to Mr. H. K. Noyes by his Dealer Organization. 1920–1921."

"The talent exhibited by this bench is astonishing," Steele told me. "Right down to the flaring nostrils on the horses, the exactitude is truly remarkable. It is clearly a rare, one-of-a kind piece."

The Takeaway

There are several layers to this museum. Car buffs will definitely enjoy the pageant of vehicles on display in the Larz Anderson collection. The director and his staff keep this museum alive with a series of revolving displays and public events. The car shows on the carriage house grounds are popular and well-attended.

But to me the most remarkable aspect of the museum is the carriage house itself. It is stately, grand, massive, elegant, and eloquent all at once. Built in 1888 by Edmund Wheelwright, one of New England's most important architects of the era, it has been called one of the most magnificent surviving carriage houses from the period in America. The building is the blank page upon which is written so many rich stories. The stories of wealth and privilege, the stories of old money and Old Boston, the stories of a couple famously in love with each other and with collecting. It is a time capsule of sorts, a snow globe of Victoriana that remains intact for all of us to explore and experience.

This is a great museum.

The Nuts and Bolts

Larz Anderson Auto Museum

15 Newton Street
Brookline, Massachusetts 02445
(617) 522-6547
www.larzanderson.org
This museum is handicapped accessible.

Travel Suggestion

Newton Avenue is a winding road through a residential area. The sign for the museum is difficult to see. Once you enter the grounds, however, you will find a sweeping park that is popular with visitors. Parking can be found outside the carriage house front entrance.

Museum Hours

Tuesday through Sunday, 10 a.m. to 4 p.m.

Admission

Adults: $10.00
Seniors, military, and children (6–12): $5.00

Up around the Bend

Plan on spending some time enjoying the sprawling Larz Anderson Park. In 2001, the town of Brookline invested hundreds of thousands of dollars in an effort to bring this park back to its former glory. Near the top is an ice skating rink. The footprint where the Anderson's mansion once stood is now a landscaped lawn affording a view of the Boston skyline. Another fine building of note is seen directly across from the Larz Anderson Museum. The Brookline Historical Society manages the Putterham School building, which is over two centuries old and is open for tours on select dates.

The Plumbing Museum, Watertown, MA by Randy Duchaine/Alamy Stock Photo.

12 The Plumbing Museum

~~~

Watertown

First, the rumor. No, Thomas Crapper did not invent the toilet.

"Oh, no," Linda Veiking told me. She is the director of the Plumbing Museum. "Many people think so, probably because he did have a part in the early evolution of toilets, and partly, of course, because of the allure of his last name," she said. "Another Englishman named John Harrington, the godson of Queen Elizabeth I, gets the credit for that. Also, that's where the nickname 'the john' came from. It is all in the name," she smiled.

The Plumbing Museum is fun. Housed in an 1870s former ice house, the museum is remarkably beautiful. Plain brick walls extend up two stories inside the exhibit space. Old pipes are left exposed, and the tall warehouse doors where ice purveyors would load up their horse-drawn wagons are still in evidence. They have even left an ice chute exactly where it was.

"They would literally shoot out eighty-pound blocks of ice from this hole, and workers would toss them on to the waiting wagons. It was very hard work.

"Originally this was all a collection of plumbing items owned by the Charles Manoog family in Worcester. They owned a large plumbing company and apparently never threw anything out. They collected and saved everything," Veiking said. "Tubs, toilets, old pipes, sinks and more. Eventually their son got the collection and opened up a museum called the American Sanitary Plumbing Museum in Worcester. When they retired, the collection was acquired by the PHCC [Plumbing, Heating, and Cooling Contractors] of Greater Boston and the J. C. Cannistraro family, under then president J. C. Cannistraro, Jr., here in Watertown. They are a major mechanical contractor dealing in the trades. In fact, I have worked for them for many years. They own this old ice house. They renovated it, brought all the items in here, and asked me to be the curator of what we now simply call the Plumbing Museum. Best job I have ever had!"

There is a whole hierarchy of sanitary and plumbing artifacts on display here. But it is obvious that toilets are king.

"We always start our tour with the toilets. Some people blush, others giggle, but all are fascinated by our collection of historic toilets. We begin with one of the earliest toilets, made around 1860, and known as an Earth Closet. It still works. As you can see it provides a comfortable seat for the user, and a series of levers which when employed sifts ashes over the contents of the bowl. After, the bowl would be emptied in a garden or field and used as fertilizer. Older folks who take the tour nod with recognition when we get to the old toilets with the water boxes above. It was all gravity fed by pulling a chain and releasing the water. Lots of our senior visitors remember these, as they were very popular, especially in the urban areas of the early twentieth century."

As we walked down a row of water closet toilets, I noticed two things. The wooden seats got better and better, and the water boxes got higher and higher.

"Well, wood was thought to be the perfect substance for a toilet seat in the beginning. It was attractive, it expanded and contracted, it was hardy, and wood was plentiful. But eventually it proved to be a problem. Over a long period of time it dried out, cracked, and then would pinch the user. So better woods, harder woods were always being tried out. And eventually it went to the smoother, cleaner porcelain seat and, ultimately, the plastic seats used today. As for the boxes getting taller, well, the old saying was 'the higher the box, the better the flush.'"

I commented on how some of these everyday fixtures were actually quite beautiful.

"Sure, some are real works of art. Take this one for example. It is a beautiful earthenware toilet bowl called the Nautilus. It has Greek designs on it and was painted in hues of green and white. Remember, only a few people had indoor toilets when this one was made, around 1891. So, as a mark of social ranking, people would want you to see their bathrooms. They would say, 'Oh, please stay and use our toilet.' The bathroom was a grand room, always well-appointed. A room to be seen. A room to show off."

Despite her subject matter, Veiking never stoops to the scatological. Everything is very polite, both in her examples and language. It would be easy for her to resort to crude jokes as we walked along lines of toilets, chamber pots, bidets, and sitz baths. "Not only do I find this all so interesting, but it is also historic. Remember, poor sanitary condition doomed millions of people to an early death over the centuries, so what we see here, what I try and illustrate for everybody, is that, yes, it is just a toilet, but it is also an important health appliance as well."

The rest of the modern, attractive museum showcases sinks, old pipes, plumbing tools, and toilet paper ("you can't have one without the other"). We see a manmade copper sink from 1920, a silver-lined sink, a nickel-plated sink, one made of soapstone and used as an early washtub, and one hand-blown glass sink from Germany. We also find a 1926 electric dishwasher (the first year they were made), one of those ubiquitous 1950s avocado green appliances, and a 1945 Maytag wringer washing machine.

"My mother, who is now ninety-four, had one of those. She thought she was the queen of the neighborhood," the director told me.

But, as I said, clearly the toilet reigns here. From the earliest ash-sifting kind to toilets that look like they are from a modern sci-fi movie, they are all here.

"Look at this one, Chuck," Veiking said as we walked to the end of the toilet timeline. "This one has a funny story to it. One day David Kohler came to the museum. I was shocked. He is, of course, the head of one of the largest plumbing manufacturers in the world. I gave him a tour and at the end of the 'toilet section,' I showed him a new, modern Japanese toilet that we had on display. He asked me why we didn't have an American toilet here instead. I had no answer. But he did. He quickly arranged to have the Japanese toilet replaced with a Kohler Numi toilet, which we see here. It is the most sophisticated of all of our toilets."

The demonstration of this toilet alone is worth the price of admission. As Veiking works the computer control panel, the toilet assesses that I am a man standing in front of it and automatically lifts its lid. With each keypad punch the toilet transforms itself into a toilet, a bidet, a front wash, a back wash, a spray (trickle or pulse), and more. You can also accompany yourself on the Numi with Bluetooth capabilities, a radio, and ambient mood lighting. Thomas Crapper, I mean, John Harrington would be proud!

Wow Factor

"That would be what we call 'The Wall.'"

"The Wall" is a brilliant demonstration of how plumbing works in a typical two-story house. It covers the whole back wall of the museum and shows a life-sized cutaway diagram of an ordinary house showing nothing but the plumbing.

"People love this," Veiking commented, "and so do I. You see sinks, tubs, toilets, hot water heaters in the basement, water reclamation tanks on the outside, all the pipes. Just everything. And water runs through it all. Everything is labeled and installed on the wall according to plumbing codes. It really brings it all to life."

It is an incredible display and definitely one of a kind. In fact, with the push of a button, Veiking started a rainstorm that began water flowing through the pipes!

The Takeaway

For readers of this book who have ever taken a charter motor coach trip, you will know what I mean by a "Secret Stop." This is usually an unannounced stop along your trip that is a bonus treat for you and your fellow travelers. I have been on dozens of these trips. If ever there was a perfect Secret Stop, this would be it. The Plumbing Museum is fun, important, entertaining, beautiful, unusual, and very surprising.

The Nuts and Bolts

The Plumbing Museum

80 Rosedale Road
Watertown, Massachusetts 02471
(617) 926-2111
www.theplumbingmuseum.org
This museum is handicapped accessible.

Travel Suggestion

The museum can be hard to spot even though it sports a large sign. It is enveloped by several large brick buildings, which house the Cannistraro Plumbing, Heating, and HVAC Company. Once you are on Rosedale Avenue you will find it. The street is only two blocks long. Free parking is in front of the museum.

Museum Hours

Monday through Friday, by appointment only

Admission

Free

Up around the Bend

Follow Belmont Street in Watertown east about three miles to Mount Auburn Cemetery. This is one of the most famous cemeteries in Massachusetts. Notable burials here include Mary Baker Eddy, Oliver Wendell Holmes, Julia Ward Howe ("Battle Hymn of the Republic"), Henry Wadsworth Longfellow, and Marjorie Newell Robb, the last first-class passenger on the *Titanic* to die (1992).

13 Spellman Museum of Stamps and Postal History

Weston

"If there is a topic or subject matter that has not been featured on a stamp, I don't know what it would be," said Henry Lukas. He is the director of education at the Spellman Museum of Stamps and Postal History. "We have over two million philatelic items at the museum, and they cover everything from common, every-day postal items to rare, one-of-a-kind stamps. We also house an extensive library relating to postal history."

The museum is named after its driving force, Francis Cardinal Spellman (1889–1967). "Cardinal Spellman was an inveterate stamp collector, and he really amassed a significant collection. During World War II, he was the vicar of the U.S. Army, and that

Photograph by Beck. Available at: https://blogs.umass.edu/bikehara/2015/09/26 /visiting-the-spellman-museum-in-weston/.

role took him to the four corners of the world. He collected stamps wherever he went. He was very well connected. Some called him the 'American Pope,' and he was friends with both Presidents Roosevelt and Eisenhower and many other world leaders."

George Norton, the museum curator, told me that the Spellman collection makes up just a small portion of the museum's philatelic holdings. "We have many private collections here as well as those that have basically just walked in the front door. We have stamp collections from the estates of President Eisenhower, General Matthew Ridgway, Theodore Steinway (of the piano family), and others. We even have stamps from President Franklin Roosevelt's collection. He was maybe America's most famous stamp collector at the time. And although the cardinal's collection makes up just a tiny portion of the museum, we are indebted to him for getting this museum started in the first place. Cardinal Spellman was born in Whitman, Massachusetts, and he was instrumental in getting the collection and the library of the National Postal Museum moved from Philadelphia to Weston. Regis College donated an acre of land on the campus for us, and we opened our doors here on May 4, 1963, the cardinal's birthday. Over 1,500 people attended our grand opening."

The museum is a marvel of miniature art and design. There is one large exhibit room lined with wall-to-wall display cases. The collection is vast and only a portion of it can be shown at one time. The remainder is kept in an imposing vault in the basement. On the day I was there, escorted by the knowledgeable Messrs. Lukas and Norton, I could quickly identify each thematic display from the excellent signage and interesting graphics. I saw an exhibit, for example, that explained the Boston Post Road, "America's First Information Highway," which ran between Boston and New York. In this showcase were original letters that the famous Colonial Post Riders carried, men in flashy outfits who rode on horseback along the road stopping just outside each town to blast away on a long post horn to let the townsfolk know that the mail was coming. I commented to Lukas that there were no stamps to be seen on these letters. "That's right. Stamps were not invented yet," he said. Stamps were invented in England in 1840.

Another very interesting exhibit was titled "Stamps Go to War." The visitor can view mailed letters representing wars going back two centuries.

"One thing common in war postal history is the artwork and graphics on the envelopes that depict the enemy as evildoers. Mean, despicable representations showing the enemy as Satan, rats, or even monsters. We have stamps from both World Wars, Desert Storm, and as far back as the Civil War. We even have letters that were mailed during the 1870 Siege of Paris. And that was no easy feat. Paris was surrounded by Prussian troops, and the mail had to be flown up and over the enemy forces in giant hot air balloons. Return mail was sealed in large zinc balls and floated down the Seine River where French soldiers would fish the globes out of the water. I guess you could call that the first underwater mail," Norton said.

The "Road to the White House" exhibit shows stamps and first-day covers representing a number of presidential campaigns. It even includes several first ladies and vice presidents who were honored with commemorative stamps, as well as envelopes mailed on inauguration days.

The collection of Theodore Steinway is particularly interesting. "Mr. Steinway collected, among other things, music stamps. And he was also an autograph collector so he married the two into hand-made beautiful displays. Steinway, the grandson of the founder of Steinway pianos, collected every stamp in the world that was related to composers, music, drums, strings, and more," Lukas said.

One page in this exhibit has a photo and signed autograph of the virtuoso Jascha Heifetz. It shows a piece of hand-drawn (by

Steinway) sheet music accompanied by a violin stamp and the auto-graph of violinist. My favorite, however, was the Franz Liszt display, which again includes a hand-drawn music score, a rare stamp, and the actual autograph of the famous nineteenth-century Hungarian composer and pianist. It includes a signed letter from Liszt to Stein-way recommending the sale of a piano to one of his students.

I asked Lukas about a typical visitor to the museum. "Well, it is hard to say really. Many people my age remember a time when everybody collected stamps. I did. My friends all did. I did it because I loved history, and in fact went on to teach history in schools for many years. You could buy collectible stamps at virtu-ally every variety store. So we do get a lot of that. People coming in and saying, 'I remember that stamp,' or 'My grandfather had stamps just like that.' We get that a lot. And it is nice."

Wow Factor

When I asked the curator what his wow factor was at a museum with millions of little things to choose from, I was surprised at how quickly he answered.

Yes, it was a postal item. A little stamped picture postcard.

"It is really nothing special to look at," Norton began. It was a photo of a young girl that was stamped and mailed from Ireland to London during World War II. "But it has always moved me. The photo card was mailed from a mother to her young daughter. It was a dreadful time in England during the war. But the little card survived the London Blitz. And so did the little girl. She had kept the photo card all these years and walked into our museum one day and gave it to us. The story is so poignant, sad, and telling. There is an interactive online map of London today, and you can type in an address and see where every bomb landed during the Blitz from 1940 to 1941. You can find her address. It was a neighborhood down by the London docks. It was totally destroyed. The stamp on the card is unspectacular. Very common, maybe worth a fraction of a penny. But the message, the photograph, the postal markings, and the story are, to me, extraordinary."

The Takeaway

The museum is an excursion into a wonderful cornucopia of art, history, collecting, graphic design, transportation history, Americana, pop culture, and more. And I give the staff here, particularly Lukas and Norton, great credit for keeping the art of stamp collecting and postal history alive. They work hard to make a connection with young people, and I commend them for their efforts. They like to say here, "You don't have to be a stamp collector to enjoy the museum."

I mentioned that my wife was a schoolteacher and that if she told her class they were going to a stamp museum for a fieldtrip, she would be met with a collective groan. How does the Stamp Museum handle a youth group?

I am here to tell you that they handle it brilliantly.

"We bring the kids into the library and give them all a postcard," Lukas began. "We tell them to address it to themselves and write a note on it. Most look up and say 'we don't know how to do that.' We show them the proper way to address a postcard or envelope. Then we let them pick out their own stamp to mail it with. It is funny to watch them try and pound the stamps on the cards. They had never heard of having to lick a stamp to affix it to the mail. After a brief tour and discussion, we bring them back in and show them boxes and boxes of stamps representing every aspect of life. We tell them to pick out several. They go wild for them, picking out animal stamps, doll stamps, sports stamps, and any others they may be interested in. And then, we let them take them home. And of course, in a day or two they receive the postcard that they wrote

and mailed to themselves. They love it. I mean, how many other museums let you actually go home with something?" he laughed.
   Brilliant.

The Nuts and Bolts

Spellman Museum of Stamps and Postal History
241 Wellesley Street
Weston, Massachusetts 02493
(781) 768-8367
www.spellmanmuseum.org
This museum is handicapped accessible.

Travel Suggestion
The museum is located on the campus of Regis College.

Museum Hours
Thursday through Sunday, 12 p.m. to 5 p.m., or by appointment

Admission
Adults: $8.00
Seniors: $5.00
Children (5–16): $3.00

Up around the Bend

Weston is a lovely New England community. It is one of the ten most affluent small towns in America. One of the highlights of a visit to Weston is the arboretum known as the Case Estates. In 1911, one of the owners, Marian Roby Case, had a wall constructed around the botanical garden. At ten feet tall and six feet thick, it has been called the largest freestanding stone wall in America.

14 Golden Ball Tavern Museum

∽

Weston

What a remarkable structure this is. The Golden Ball Tavern has been located on the Boston Post Road for over 250 years. It is one of the few museums in Massachusetts that brings to life the Loyalist experience before the American Revolution in exciting detail.

Oh, if these old walls could talk.

"This is such a historic and evocative building," Joan Bines, the museum's director, told me. "It tells of the original owner Isaac Jones's moral dilemma as he struggled to choose sides before and during the war, and then it continues on through time with the stories of six more generations of his family who lived here.

"I am passionately in love with this place and its integrity. I have a Ph.D. in history, and this is the real deal. Understanding this house is like trying to understand a mystery. It is a detective story with many twists and turns. This house bears witness to so many events in American history. For instance, Paul Revere and a large contingent of his soldiers stopped here for breakfast in August of 1777 on their way from Boston to Worcester to bring back a group of British prisoners of war. It must have been quite a scene. After the visit, the owner's wife, Mary, accused Revere and his men of stealing twelve loaves of sugar—sugar during the war being a valuable commodity."

I asked Bines about the building's earliest configuration as a tavern.

"There were four taverns along this important road. The Golden Ball was the most popular. Here, Isaac Jones and his family entertained visitors in a style one man wrote was 'the most convenient of any along the road. . . . The rooms are commodious, provisions good and servants attentive.' Jones and others basically held court here. In colonial days a tavern would be the only heated communal meeting place; a center for gatherings; an inn; a place for drink, meals, and overnight stays; a focal point for political gatherings; or just a place to gossip and catch up on the local news. The tavern served beer, rum, cider, punch, coffee, and tea. And it was the tea that got the tavern and its owner in trouble."

Britain's onerous taxes, duties, and restrictions imposed on the American colonies in the late 1760s and early 1770s led the colonists to fear the loss of their liberties. Parliament's insistence on taxing all tea exported to the colonies became a powerful symbol of Britain's intent to tax the colonists without their consent. Jones, however, continued to serve tea in clear defiance of his more patriotic neighbors.

"It was a difficult time for Isaac. His heart was with the British, not because he believed that they were right in all their actions, but he remembered all the things about the British that were good and positive. The British constitution was the envy of the world, securing individual rights that no people outside the British Empire enjoyed. Parliament may have acted rashly, but Jones thought rebellion was not the answer. Instead, he advocated compromise. Because of this, one night in 1774, while he was away, a mob of over three hundred patriots from Weston and beyond, their faces painted like Indians, ransacked the Golden Ball looking for Isaac to punish him. They smashed doors and windows and stole raisins, lemons, and liquor all the while Mary cowered upstairs in her bed with her newborn baby. Everybody has heard of the Boston Tea Party, but few have heard of the Weston Tea Party."

Despite such actions, Isaac Jones remained a "friend of government." When British general Thomas Gage's spies happened upon the tavern in February 1775, they were quite relieved when their host offered them "what they might please, either tea or coffee." They wrote, "It was then that we were pleased to find that he was a friend of government."

Bines continued, "We do know that Jones eventually became a patriot because there is evidence of him hauling supplies to New York for the American side."

The Golden Ball Tavern has what architects call "good bones." It was built to be both a private and a public place. Many of the original features of this centuries-old building are still on display. "Jones's small, upstairs personal office still has the original fireplace, and above it a ledger cabinet built into the wall with cubbies for papers and account books. Isaac sat at this desk, smoking his clay pipe, watching the traffic on the Post Road below. We know this because we have found handfuls of clay pipe stems poked into the small opening of the window sill. Another clue!"

"The paint is called Prussian Blue. It was very expensive and rare at the time, and even though it is a little worn we decided not to replace it so as to allow the house to tell its own story."

Throughout the structure, wherever possible, clear plastic panels have been placed over floors and walls so that visitors can see the original wood, paint, and wallpaper. Some of the doors on the second floor ingeniously can be raised on hooks forming a small ballroom where patrons could dance or meet. In the main floor kitchen, which dates back to 1768, a part of the huge walk-in hearth has been left exposed to see the original flues underneath the bricks. Papers, documents, and ephemera throughout tell the story of the tavern's history, including a copy of the Golden Ball's original liquor license dated from 1770 through the Revolution.

Bines remarked, "So you see, even though his loyalties were suspect at times, this town loved and respected Isaac Jones. He was a serious and intelligent man. We do know that in 1913, Weston historian Daniel S. Lamson wrote, 'Captain Isaac Jones filled a much larger space in the history of the town than perhaps any other inhabitant before or since.'"

Wow Factor

"No question about it. The Latten Spoons," the director said. "Follow me."

Bines opened an old creaky door, and we went down a long set of wooden steps into the ancient basement of the building (this is not a part of the museum tour because of safety concerns). As I descended the steps behind her, I noticed that many of the old beams supporting the walls were labeled or numbered. This was an old process of putting together a building as if it were a puzzle. The basement itself has a dirt floor and a ten-foot ceiling. The dim lighting and damp smell told me that we were on our way to something mysterious.

"Look at the walls here," she said, rubbing her hands over the large stone foundation. "These are original, can you imagine? Well, years ago when repairs were being made, some of the stones needed to be replaced. When removing them, three spoons inexplicably fell out of the wall." She showed me the spoons.

They were Latten Spoons, commonly used in the 1600s and made out of an alloy of copper and zinc. They resemble brass. Each has a flat stem and a shallow bowl at the end. They were usually used by the cooks or domestics of the household until they outlived their usefulness and were thrown away. They are considered a rare find in today's antiques world.

"These three spoons. Why are they here? Obviously, Isaac placed them into the foundation to be found later. In this case much later. Centuries later. I have been involved with the Golden Ball for over thirty years, and these are my treasures. They just give the place such a connection to Isaac. He put them there. To me these spoons represent everything about the man. His convictions, his beliefs, his connectedness to everything around him. It is as if he put these three spoons in the wall almost as a blessing on this foundation of the home, which served his family well for hundreds of years."

As I watched Bines caress these spoons in the dimly lit shadows of this ancient room, the significance of the Golden Ball really came to me.

"Just three small spoons," she said. "Why were they in the wall? We will never know. But to me they are alive. They represent the love of his ancestors."

The Takeaway

Massachusetts has no shortage of great and grand old houses with amazing backstories. The Golden Ball Tavern ranks among the best of these. It is hard to capture a takeaway aspect of the tavern in one or two sentences. It was all so interesting.

One clue to the enormity of the story at the Golden Ball is a display of items found over the years on the grounds. Six archaeological digs have taken place on the tavern property over the years, and a fine collection of their results is on display in a large case. Here you can see bits of china, an old mug, a child's shoe, some oyster shells (which is curious since Weston is about twenty miles inland), a straight razor, clay pipes, a doll, farm tools, and more. It is a fascinating, unique window into the lives of those who lived in this house over the last 250 years.

And don't leave until you ask to see the Latten Spoons!

The Nuts and Bolts

Golden Ball Tavern Museum

662 Boston Post Road
Weston, Massachusetts 02493
(781) 894-1751
www.goldenballtavern.org
Contact the museum for handicapped accessibility.

Travel Suggestion

Just west of Weston look for a sign for the museum at the corner of Route 20 and Golden Ball Road. The museum is two blocks away. Turn onto Golden Ball Road and then right on the Old Post Road.

Museum Hours

The museum is open by appointment only. It frequently holds "free open houses" on the second Sunday of each month, which do not require an appointment. Check the website for information.

Admission

Free

Up around the Bend

An unusual landmark in this area is the Norumbega Tower. This fieldstone tower was erected by Eben Norton Horsford in 1889 to mark what was reported to be an ancient Norse village. The tower is forty feet tall and has a spiral staircase inside that takes you to a small observation deck at the top. It is located on Norumbega Road just east of I-95 at the confluence of Stony Brook and the Charles River.

15 The International Museum of World War II

Natick

This is not the easiest museum to find. There is no sign out front. The only thing that distinguishes it as a museum about war is the piece of vintage artillery on the front lawn. You have to press a buzzer to enter the front door. It is only open by appointment. A waiver must be signed before you enter the exhibit area. And then, and only then, are you allowed in for a tour of the International Museum of World War II.

Despite all of the intrigue in getting inside, it is well worth it. I have been to a lot of World War II museums, both in the United States and abroad, and this is by far one of the best.

I began my visit by chatting with Marshall Carter, the director of education for the museum. He is passionate, animated, interesting, and a veritable encyclopedia of World War II history. We met in the "workroom."

"As you can see all around you," he began, "we have a lot of material here. In fact, we have over a half million different items pertaining to the World War II era. Obviously, we don't have room to display them all at once, but we are able to display up to eight thousand items at a time. It is pretty incredible."

I looked around the room, which is basically a warehouse of catalogued World War II items. Each of the hundreds of gray boxes is labeled. "Japan P.O.W." "German Children." "U.S. Cargo Items." "French Occupation." "Military Medals." "Concentration Camps." The list went on and on. I picked a box at random and asked Carter if I could see the inside of it. I chose a box labeled "Paris Newsboy Shoes."

"Well, here they are," he said, as he gingerly opened up the box. And sure enough it was a pair of brown leather shoes. Just a pair of shoes.

"Someone brought them in to us, and we have them here ready to exhibit, perhaps for a display on what life was like on the streets of Paris during the war. Of course, like anything else in the museum, this is not merely a pair of shoes. This is a story. Someone's actual story," he said as he returned the shoes to the box.

The museum is laid out smartly. In chronological order, Carter guided me from one stage of the World War II era to the next, beginning in the prewar rooms. "It is important that we set the stage for the war by showing, in documents and artifacts, what the state of Germany, and Europe as a whole, was like just before war broke out. We are the only World War II museum in the world to present it as a global event. We are about the causes and consequences of war. It is hard to imagine the hardships the war created all over the world. Like the newsboy's shoes, for example. Let's face it, if you lived in France in 1941, your life was the war."

The displays in each room are dazzling. Powerful propaganda

posters line virtually every wall. Flags and banners float above your head. Old newspaper headlines blare out the creeping grasp of power by Adolf Hitler and his Third Reich. Colorful uniforms stand sentinel on mute mannequins. I recognized a lot of them. The Eisenhower jacket. Churchill's gray, pinstriped suit. A GI helmet. The dreaded black uniform of the S.S. with the silver skulls on the caps.

We eventually reach the years when America entered the war. "This is where many of our visitors really connect with our collection. We have thousands of American items that they, or maybe a family member, either saw, used, had, or were familiar with. We have some great military vehicles scattered throughout the museum too, including a standard U.S. military Jeep, a 1942 Sherman M-42, and more. Outside, we have an actual Higgins boat. These were the ubiquitous landing craft that Eisenhower called 'the boat that won the war.' There are less than a dozen known Higgins boats in existence, out of more than twenty thousand made, and ours is one of them."

The collection is absolutely Smithsonian in scope. The signed documents alone are worth the visit. "Yes, we are fortunate to have so much original correspondence from the war. And of course we cover both theaters of the war. We have an actual print of Joe Rosenthal's famous Iwo Jima flag-raising photograph. It was developed while he was still on Guam. We have letters written by Japanese prime minister Tojo from his postwar jail cell. One of my favorites is a telegram with the words 'Play Ball' on it. A young officer delivered this telegram from General Eisenhower to General George Patton using the code words meaning that the invasion of North Africa was a go. Patton turned around and handed the telegram back to the officer and said, 'Here you keep this, son. It is going to be a souvenir someday.' And we have it."

The French Resistance Room is absorbing. We see all types of subterfuge the citizens of France used to thwart the occupying Germans. There is a small baby carriage that classically exemplifies this. The baby buggy looks typical in every way, but as Carter showed me, if you lifted up the child's mattress, there was a secret compartment for a radio. "This way the woman could walk all over the streets of her French town smuggling a clandestine radio without drawing attention to herself."

The Holocaust Room is appropriately somber and claustrophobic. Concentration camp uniforms, yellow Star of David patches, guard uniforms, gas chamber items, and more tell the familiar and grim story of the plight of Europe's Jews and other "enemies" of the Third Reich. A letter from Otto Frank, dated August 1945, speaks of his hope of keeping his daughter Anne's memory alive.

I mentioned to Carter that for a World War II fanatic like me, this visit was like living a dream. The sheer magnitude of the items is overwhelming. The actual chair Hitler sat in in his jail cell while writing *Mein Kampf*. A pair of deck binoculars from the doomed USS *Arizona*. The uniforms of the famous Tuskegee Airmen pilots. The telegram coming from headquarters at Pearl Harbor on December 7, 1941, declaring in all capital letters, "THIS IS NOT A DRILL!" U.S downed pilots' escape routes printed on silk handkerchiefs. Poet Robert Frost's personal signed wartime ration card. British prime minister Neville Chamberlain's actual plane ticket from his fateful flight back from Munich to announce "peace in our time." A French woman's wedding dress fashioned out of an American silk parachute.

"We also have one of the world's largest collections of German Enigma coding machines," Carter said as he led me to a long table. Nine of the machines were lined up. "We encourage our visitors to use the keyboards to see how they really worked. Others have these machines, but we are the only place where we allow people to use them."

Wow Factor

When I asked Carter what his wow factor was, he made a beeline right back to the workroom where we started. Here he picked up a child's sewing kit.

"This is a small item, but a powerful one. It comes from a little girl in France. Her name was Mauricette."

When we opened it, we saw all the typical accoutrements of a child's sewing kit: yarn, buttons, scissors, crochet patterns, and a little doll. "We know that Mauricette carried secret messages in the bottom of her sewing kit. It is not known whether or not she realized she was doing this dangerous work. It is just so illustrative of how the home front was also a battlefront for so many people. This little girl was an unwitting soldier in the conflict even though she was only about ten years old. It reminds us about the horrors of war. It is poignant. It is an utterly ordinary object which tells us an extraordinary human story about war."

The Takeaway

For those interested in World War II, this museum is as good as it gets. The size of the priceless collection is astounding, and it is no wonder that a major expansion project is now under way which will allow for a larger public mission. Surprises are around every turn. The story of the war is told in excruciating detail. So many of the items are remarkable due to the fact that they are absolutely original to the era.

The best way to describe the flow of the museum, the room-to-room timeline, are three letters I saw in a display case in the D-Day Invasion Room. These letters illuminate the fact that with this mighty invasion, the tide of war was finally about to turn.

The missives include the first postinvasion letters exchanged between each of the two warring generals and their respective wives. Eisenhower's letter to his beloved Mamie begins with, "My Darling. Anyway we have started!" In contrast, the first letter written by German Field Marshal Erwin Rommel to his wife, Lucia, begins darkly: "My dear, I am afraid a lot of hardship has been let out."

And beside those two men's letters, young Anne Frank writes of the very same day: "Great commotion in the 'Secret Annex!' Would the long awaited liberation that has been talked of so much, but which seems too wonderful, too much like a fairy tale, ever come true? Could we be granted victory this year, 1944?"

Chilling.

The Nuts and Bolts

The International Museum of World War II
8 Mercer Road
Natick, Massachusetts 01760
(508) 651-1944
www.museumofworldwarii.org
This museum is handicapped accessible.

Travel Suggestion
The museum is located behind the Sherwood Plaza Shopping Center.

Museum Hours

Fridays and Saturdays, 9 a.m. to 4 p.m., or by appointment
You must sign and bring the security and release waiver form that can only be found at the website. This form states the rules of the museum, including acknowledgment that there are many weapons and sharp items on display that visitors should be cautious of. All are non-working, original weapons used in World War II.

Admission

Adults: $25.00
Seniors: $20.00
Children (with accompanying adult): $15.00

Up around the Bend

No visit to Natick is complete without a stop at Casey's Diner for one of its famous steamed hot dogs. The diner is one of the oldest ten-stool diners in the United States, built in 1922. It is fun and delicious but a tight squeeze. Casey's measures only ten by twenty feet. It is located at 36 South Avenue, Natick.

REGION THREE
Southeast

Photograph by Kenneth C. Zirkel. Creative Commons license available at:
https://creativecommons.org/licenses/by-sa/4.0/.

16 Lizzie Borden Bed and Breakfast/ Museum

Fall River

The Borden residence at 230 Second Street in Fall River is a sturdy, green shuttered building not without a large degree of grace and charm. It stands erect among the newer neighboring structures, an architectural souvenir of a past era. Inside, the house is beautifully appointed in Victorian-era accoutrements, furnishings, wall hangings, and paraphernalia. It has a peaceful ambience, albeit a bit stuffy, and exudes an appropriate air that recalls when the owner of the home, Andrew Borden, stood among the ranks of the wealthy and prominent citizenry of this manufacturing city. "Lovely" is the perfect word to describe this abode, which held Andrew and his second wife, Abby, and his two daughters, Emma and Lizzie. An Irish maid, Bridget, lived in an attic loft.

How then is it possible that this quiet domicile could have been turned into a blood-drenched house of horror in a matter of minutes on the morning of Thursday, August 4, 1892?

"Nobody will ever know the answer to that," tour guide Richard Bertoldo told me. "After more than a century, it is still one of the great crime mysteries of all time."

Bertoldo gave me a private two-hour tour of the mansion. He is an expert with few peers on the Lizzie Borden story.

"I first got interested when I was a kid. My school in New Bedford was the Hosea M. Knowlton High School. To us kids it was just a name. One day I decided to find out just who this Hosea Knowlton really was. I discovered that not only was he a politician of note, but he was also the lead prosecutor in the Lizzie Borden axe murder case. That really caught my attention, and I have been fascinated by the case ever since."

Bertoldo spun a dramatic tale of mystery and murder as he took me from room to room, all the while keeping up a steady patter of facts, opinions, and folklore. In the old-fashioned kitchen he pointed to the door where the killer must have entered if he or she was not already in the house. In the parlor he described the minute-by-minute happenings of every major occupant in the house that day in 1892. He told me of the rise of Andrew Borden from a working man with no funds to one of the pillars of Fall River society. He also opined that Borden was a skinflint.

"Andrew Borden made a lot of money. In fact, when he died the amount of his fortune would be in the millions in today's figures. But he was as cheap as they come. Despite all the embellishments he made to this beautiful home, he still never put in indoor plumbing. He had a two-stall privy put in the basement for everybody to use. Each bedroom had its own chamber pot under the bed," Bertoldo noted.

As the tour of the main floor continued, he became quieter as he reached the end of the timeline. With a flair he thumped the table loudly with his hand, signifying the sound that must have been made by Abby Borden's body slumping to the floor in the bedroom just above our heads. He then led me up the stairs.

"Stop on the seventh stair and look to your left," he whispered as we ascended the wooden staircase. At the seventh step I looked to the left.

"Here is where the first sighting of the dead woman's body could be noticed. Under the slit in the door, Mrs. Borden's body would have clearly been seen by anyone reaching this seventh step. She would've been in a sitting position and was drenched in blood. She had been hit in the head with an axe nineteen times. She was a bloody pulp," the tour guide continued.

All the while Lizzie was "discovering" her dead stepmother lying in a bloody heap upstairs, her father, Andrew, was lying dead on the parlor couch downstairs. He too was butchered, having been hit in the back of the head seventeen times with an axe. The discovery of his body set things in motion.

Bedlam ensued.

"Remember, with no killer in custody, the city was seized with the fear that an axe murderer was on the loose. The bodies of the two dead people remained in this house for three days while the investigation went on. Lizzie swore to the police that she didn't do it, and the only other suspects were a male visitor who stayed over the night before but was long gone and the Irish maid who was quickly eliminated as a suspect. The trial gripped the city of Fall River. In fact, it drew the attention of the entire nation. The story of the double axe murder and the sympathetic Lizzie had all the ingredients of a real pot-boiler. It has been said that the Borden murder trial was the first such major case to have international appeal due to the recent advent of newspaper wire service techniques. People all over the world followed the day-by-day goings-on at the trial."

At the end of the tour Bertoldo focused on the trial and its findings. Lizzie was acquitted. No substantial evidence to prove her the murderer surfaced. It was a dramatic trial accompanied by horrific crime scene and autopsy photographs, which are now displayed on the dainty, white-laced tablecloth on the dining room table. They are grisly.

"The mystery lives on," he said. "We get visitors from all over the world who come here for the tours and to see the house for itself. I have been doing the tours for years, and it still even intrigues me. I guess it always will."

Wow Factor

"Well, this item is certainly unique," Bertoldo said. In the corner of the room where Mrs. Borden was killed stands an eerie mannequin. It looks lifelike and is quite startling when first noticed behind the bedroom door. "The dress on this mannequin is the same one worn by actress Elizabeth Montgomery in the 1975 television movie *The Legend of Lizzie Borden*. Obviously, it is a one of a kind."

A photograph of the actress in this dress on the set of the movie is featured next to the mannequin.

It adds just the right dose of creepiness to the whole dark, fascinating tour of the house.

The Takeaway

We have all heard the childhood rhyme about Lizzie Borden giving her mother and father those mortal "whacks with an axe." But to actually see, in great detail, the backstory to that famous murder is really exceptional. It is unique to all the museums I have been. As if preserved in a time capsule, the Lizzie Borden house, and her fine interpreters, will keep this absorbing story alive for many generations to come. It is a fascinating place, a great story, and an exciting tour.

The house is an active B&B. Its overnight rooms (including the murder rooms) are booked well in advance. Reservations for the anniversary of the murder (August 4) and Halloween must be made nearly a year prior. The owners have really poured their hearts and souls into making this museum relevant today. Oh, and you will know if the owners are on premises. Just look in the parking lot for two vehicles with the license plates "FRTYWX" and "LIZZIEB."

And, yes. They do now have bathrooms!

The Nuts and Bolts

Lizzie Borden Bed and Breakfast/Museum

230 Second Street
Fall River, Massachusetts 02721
(508) 675-7333
https://lizzie-borden.com
This museum is not handicapped accessible.

Travel Suggestion

The Lizzie Borden B&B and Museum is located across the street from the back of the large Fall River Justice Center building.

Museum Hours

Tours are given daily on the hour from 11 a.m. to 3 p.m.

Admission

Adults: $20.00
Seniors (60+) and college students (with ID): $18.00
Children (7–12): $15.00

Up around the Bend

As of the publication of this book, another Lizzie Borden site will be available for viewing. After her acquittal, and much to the surprise of the residents of Fall River, Lizzie stayed in the city despite almost total ostracism. She inherited a fortune from the deaths of her parents and bought a large mansion where she lived the rest of her life. That home, Maplecroft, is expected to act as another museum and B&B documenting the latter part of Lizzie's life. Details can be found at the Lizzie Borden B&B.

17 Battleship Cove

Fall River

Battleship Cove represents the world's largest collection of preserved historic U.S. naval ships afloat. Each is its own museum, and each is more awesome than the next.

"They are huge and they are magnificent," Brad King told me. He is the executive director of the collection. "Each one represents a chapter in America's military history. The sheer scale and magnitude of the ships is breathtaking. The character of the ships alone is worth noting. They are not just standalone ships; each one has touched the lives of all sorts of people, and they still do. They are not dead things. They are very much alive. Each person who comes here adds to the history. It is just a different story. The collective impression adds up to a demonstration of the American character," he said.

And that is from a Brit, no less!

Photograph by Wikimaster97commons. Creative Commons license available at: https://creativecommons.org/licenses/by/3.0/.

King is the former director of HMS *Belfast* warship museum in London. That ship, located on Queen's Walk on the Thames, is very similar to the ships found at Battleship Cove. "I worked at the Imperial War Museum in London for nearly three decades, and was director at the *Belfast* museum for eight years. The missions of the museums are quite similar with the same type of clientele and same kind of storytelling dynamic. When this job came open I jumped at it."

Battleship Cove is made up of the USS *Massachusetts* (battleship), USS *Joseph P. Kennedy Jr.* (destroyer), USS *Lionfish* (submarine), PT Boats 617 and 796, and the Russian missile corvette *Hiddensee*. All are open to the public.

I met Director King in the mess hall of "Big Mamie," the endearing nickname of the *Massachusetts*. The ship is gargantuan, and everything about it—on top, inside, and below the water level—is restored to as close to original condition as possible. Of course, it has some dings and bruises, too. But those scars tell a dramatic story.

"As you can see, there are many red marks painted all over the walls here," King told me as we walked through the men's sleeping quarters. "Each red mark denotes an area where a piece of shrapnel from an enemy shell came blasting through." I noted that the area was liberally pockmarked with these deadly markings. I asked him how many died from these shrapnel bursts.

"None. Of course, if a battle was raging this room would be empty with all the men on top at their battle stations. The USS *Massachusetts* could hold two thousand men. It was a virtual city. And she never lost a single man in combat."

A tour of this mighty ship is a humbling experience. The massive guns, the plated turrets, the giant "binoculars" seeking out enemy ships, the steep metal staircases leading to the bowels of the ship. Everything is like a war movie set come to life.

"Many of our visitors are veterans who come back for events and reunions. They get quite sentimental roaming around this old ship. Many times there are tears. We host hundreds of students and others annually in our Nautical Nights programs. These are very popular with the young people, and they have been going on for many years. They actually come on board and sleep on the ship. It can be quite exciting for them. Even former Massachusetts governor Mitt Romney and Boston Red Sox pitcher Curt Schilling once stayed on the *Massachusetts* overnight with their families."

I asked about the other ships.

"The 'Joey P' is the only destroyer of its type in this configuration anywhere, so destroyer vets come and look around and see what memories turn up. As you know Joseph P. Kennedy, Jr., was a war hero who died on August 12, 1944. This ship was launched in 1945 so it missed any action in World War II, but it did play a part in other actions, including the Cuban Missile Crisis. The Kennedy family has really taken to the legacy of this ship and their relative. Joe's sister Jean Kennedy, who is now the last of Joe's siblings, has a real affinity for this ship and is in frequent contact," King told me.

A separate building holds the two PT boats.

"To our knowledge there are less than a dozen World War II PT boats still in existence. We have two of them. And of course, again, we have the Kennedy connection here because of President Kennedy's historic past with PT 109. In fact one of our boats, PT 796, was in President Kennedy's inaugural parade in 1961. When it was retired it had been in naval service longer than any other World War II PT boat. Because of all of these connections, we like to think of ourselves as the caretakers of the Kennedy family's military legacy."

The USS *Lionfish* did deep-sea duty throughout World War II and well into the 1960s. It rescued a large number of downed U.S. fighter pilots.

But what about the Russian ship?

"Ah, yes. The *Hiddensee*. It is rare in that it is the only communist attack ship on display and open to the public. It was once part of the East German navy, and after a circuitous route it ended up here. A funny thing happened a while back," King said. "We located the former captain of the *Hiddensee,* and he came over to Fall River for his sixtieth birthday. He came on board his old ship and remarked at what wonderful condition it was still in. He stepped into the engine room and flicked the switch and all the lights immediately came on. He told us stories about its firepower. He told us that when he was captain of the *Hiddensee,* his offensive capabilities were such that he could fire four missiles and four different targets in four directions simultaneously in under four seconds. That is pretty amazing. The best part was when we took him into his old captain's quarters. There on the wall was a large picture that he had brought from his home and hung there many years before. It was quite a moment."

Wow Factor

King walked me into a large display room on the second deck. One wall is dominated by an enormous forty-eight-star flag.

"We call this the Casablanca Flag. In November of 1942, the U.S. Navy moved on Casablanca in French Morocco. In the harbor there was a large enemy battleship, the *Jean Bart*. It was not seaworthy at the time but was fully armed and acted as a significant defense deterrent to the navy. As the *Massachusetts* was shelling the harbor, the *Jean Bart* was firing sixteen-inch shells back at her. One of them tore through this very flag leaving a hole. It was a close call. We display this flag with the hole still in it as a reminder of the military action this ship had seen."

The flag is huge, measuring ten by fifteen feet. The shell hole is quite visible. There is also an accompanying photograph taken at the end of the Battle of Casablanca with the hole very much in evidence.

The Casablanca Flag is certainly a high point on a tour of "Big Mamie."

The Takeaway

Like most baby boomer boys, I just can't get enough of battleships and wartime adventures. Battleship Cove does not disappoint. I was astonished upon entering the separate room with the two PT boats on display how large they were. In my mind's eye, they were slim, sleek, and mosquito-like in their ability to dart and dash across the ocean waves. I was struck at how really big they are. All of the other ships are equally interesting. One of the most intriguing factoids that Brad King graced me with had to do with a large shell swinging from a heavy chain.

"We keep this out here to illustrate just how powerful our weapons were. The missile swinging from this chain is an actual sixteen-inch shell from the guns of the *Massachusetts*. It weighs as much as a Toyota Corolla, could be fired at a moving target some twenty-two miles away, a target it couldn't 'see' mind you, hit it, and cause massive damage."

It is clear that King is very fond of the entire battleship complex. It is also clear to me that the USS *Massachusetts* is his favorite ship. At one point, as we stood on the deck surveying the massive steel plating and armaments, he simply looked up at the ship and said, "Amazing isn't it? A colossus that floats."

The Nuts and Bolts

Battleship Cove

5 Water Street
Fall River, Massachusetts 02721
(508) 678-1100
www.battleshipcove.org
This museum is handicapped accessible.

Travel Suggestion

With its huge guns pointing skyward, the 35,000-ton USS *Massachusetts* is hard to miss along the waterfront of Fall River. If you do need a landmark to follow, Battleship Cove is located directly underneath the soaring Braga Bridge, which connects Fall River with Somerset on the other side of the Taunton River.

Museum Hours

April 1 through October 31: Daily, 9 a.m. to 4 p.m.
November 1 through March 31: Friday to Sunday, 9 a.m. to 4 p.m.
The museum is closed Thanksgiving, Christmas, and New Year's Day.

Admission

Adults: $25.00
Seniors: $23.00
Children (4–12): $15.00

Up around the Bend

The riverfront area that hosts Battleship Cove is the site of a recent renaissance. From the battleship museum you can walk to a historic carousel, the Marine Museum at Fall River, and Fall River Heritage State Park, as well as several nice restaurants and pubs.

18 National Black Doll Museum of History and Culture

~~~

Mansfield

"As a kid I loved dolls. I was an avid doll collector. Still, I had no black dolls because my parents just couldn't find them anywhere, and if they did come upon one, it was way too expensive. I desperately wanted one that looked just like me. I vowed that if I could ever find black dolls that I would start collecting them. And I did."

And so, some six thousand black dolls later, Debra Britt is now the owner of America's largest private black doll collections. And from this collection comes a truly fascinating and inspiring little museum in Mansfield, Massachusetts.

"I change out the displays every six to eight weeks. Just to keep it interesting. I try to incorporate my love for black dolls with my interest in black American history. I visit schools, organizations and groups all the time teaching about black History and the stories of our past in this country. And I always take my dolls with me. The youngsters really enjoy that."

Barely an inch is wasted in this large storefront on Main Street. Theme rooms abound. Historic timelines are explained. Holidays are celebrated. And all with black dolls.

"In our Sports Room we feature dolls in the image of our great black sports heroes, like Muhammad Ali, Jackie Robinson, the Williams sisters, Tiger Woods, Joe Louis, Hank Aaron, and others. In the Fashion Room we find black dolls designed by the greatest names in fashion, so you know the little girls love it in there. Our Music Room highlights the contributions of African American entertainers over the years, again all with black dolls. We have a Louis Armstrong doll, Diana Ross and the Supremes dolls, Ella Fitzgerald, and so many others. Lots of stuff from Motown. All of these are my own personal dolls, and I enjoy sharing my passion for them with the public."

Of course she doesn't share them all. All at once. How could she?

"I have at least 6,000 black dolls, but honestly I stopped counting long ago," Britt said. "I have more than 500 black Santa Claus dolls, 3,000 other black holiday dolls, 200 black Cabbage Patch dolls, 1,500 black Barbie dolls, hundreds of black action dolls, and so many more. My oldest doll is an 1847 doll made out of a wishbone. I have dolls from the Jim Crow era and dolls as current as this year. And I love each and every one of them."

Britt created the Doll E. Daze nonprofit organization to get her message out to those most in need.

"One of the most powerful old stories I tell is about the Africans who came to America jammed into the holds of giant slave ships. They were treated horribly and were not allowed to have any possessions of their own. During the voyage the mothers told a story to their frightened children about keeping the faith and not losing hope. When they could they taught their children how to confront their feelings by decorating a calabash, a type of gourd, into a doll. They covered the gourd with beads and ribbons and, when possible, put a little apple head on top of the gourd to make a doll. From these gourds the slave children rejected the God of Fear and instead welcomed the God of Hopes and Dreams. The slave owners never understood these gourds and therefore let the children have them. And with that a sense of peace would be instilled in the little ones at a time of great trial. It is a wonderful story, and I tell it frequently. It even resonates with many today, and that is the basis of our Doll E. Daze Project."

She has taken her doll project into places where little light is shone. Homeless shelters, battered women's clinics, prisons, inner-city youth clubs, rape counseling centers, and others. And she always takes along "her dolls."

"I substitute plastic water bottles for gourds. I take along recycled scraps of cloth, ribbons, beads, and such. And I teach the story of the calabash dolls on the slave ships. Everybody then gets to make a doll. In doing so I encourage them to give up their fears and receive a message of hope. I have to tell you, some of their stories are harrowing. From violence to bullying to even the death of one's child, these people live in dark places. When they see the dolls that they've made, their faces just light right up. It is heartwarming."

I asked Britt what these people do with their newly made dolls.

"They treasure them. For many it is the first doll they have had. Plus, they made it themselves, they have been exposed to someone who cares for them and their problems, and they really feel a sense of release as they have unburdened themselves of their greatest fears. Often for the first time ever. Old women make the dolls, children, even men. It is miraculous."

Debra Britt is a force of nature and a guided tour with her at the doll museum is a thought-provoking, emotional, and compelling experience.

Wow Factor

"My Bob Marley doll," the owner practically squealed.

She walked me over to an eighteen-inch Bob Marley doll encased in a glass box.

"It was sculpted by Jack Johnston, one of the premier doll artists in America. Reggae star Bob Marley's mother asked him to make a doll for her in the image of her late son. He dressed the doll in remnants of Bob's actual clothes. As it neared completion he began working on the singer's face. Mrs. Marley brought the sculptor locks of Bob's very own hair that she had in a family Bible, and he fashioned them onto the doll's head. It is so special and rare. It was eventually given to me in respect for what I am doing here. I cherish it."

The doll, depicted seated on a bench, is a remarkable likeness of Bob Marley. It holds a special place in the museum's Music Room.

The Takeaway

I enjoyed this museum on several different levels, not the least being that it exists at all.

"Yes, some did not want this little black doll museum plopped right in the middle of downtown Mansfield," she said. "But I kept on keeping on. I got hate mail, with people threatening me, telling me I didn't belong here. Some told me to 'go home where I came from.' This was kind of funny since I come from here," she laughed.

There is a doll-making room here where Britt holds classes. Plus she hosts several events each year.

"We have a sleepover party for young girls that is very popular. They come in, we tell stories, I show them the dolls, they go to the workshop and make a doll to take home. We watch movies, and they sleep right here surrounded by thousands of dolls."

This is an unusual museum that really moved me. It is unique, tells a little known story in a creative way, and is both entertaining and important.

The Nuts and Bolts

National Black Doll Museum of History and Culture

288 North Main Street
Mansfield, Massachusetts 02048
(774) 284-4729
http://nbdmhc.org
This museum is handicapped accessible.

Travel Suggestion

The museum is in a storefront along Mansfield's small downtown business district. Although there are signs for it inside the front windows, there are no signs that protrude from the building denoting its location. I had to go around the block twice before I saw the museum. You'll find plenty of parking spaces out front.

Museum Hours

Thursday through Saturday, 12 p.m. to 5 p.m., and by appointment

Admission

Adults: $13.00
Seniors (55+) and youth (12–17): $9.00
Children (3–11): $6.00
Student discounts available. Group tours available.

Up around the Bend

A highway underpass in Mansfield (Route 106) holds a wonderful, colorful 325-foot long painted mural depicting much of Mansfield's history. Among the images are several geese and some gladiola greenhouses. Mansfield once had the largest goose farm in the world and also employed hundreds in the growing and selling of gladiola flowers.

19 Brockton Fire Museum

Brockton

The first thing that struck me about the Brockton Fire Museum is how beautiful it is inside. Although its exterior is sheathed entirely in plain, white New England clapboard, the bright red fire engine doors in front tip you off that the inside will be anything but, well, plain.

"This is an important museum," Ken Galligan said. He is a retired Brockton fire chief, having served as such from 1993 to 2010. "I worked for more than forty years with the city's department, and I am totally committed, along with many others, to preserving the history of firefighting in our city. Brockton is the busiest fire department in the state of Massachusetts per capita. We have had our triumphs and our tragedies, and we believe this museum is the perfect place to enshrine our history."

The museum is a showcase of colors. It is brightly lit, airy, and

roomy with gleaming pumpkin pine floors. The center of the room is taken up by several large hand-pump fire wagons that date back to the 1800s. Each is in pristine condition with shiny new coats of red paint and blinding, polished brass tubes.

"Can you imagine these things tearing through the city?" Chief Galligan said as he patted the sides of "The Protector," a hand-pumper from the early days of fire service in the city. A hand-pumper and a hand-puller.

"Remember there were no cars or trucks in those days, so these things were either pulled by horses or by hand. Once they got to the fire a corps of fifty men would gather on each side and pump the long bars on either side of the wagon. This pumping action would build up pressure, and eventually the water came shooting out. It was very hard work, and they had to work in shifts. No pumping, no water. And, of course, they had to unravel the hoses and stretch them to a water source near the fire site. A pond, river, stream anything would work. Obviously, if you lived in a house far away from a water source, you were plain out of luck. Every house was required to have a leather bucket so the regular citizenry could be marshalled for bucket brigades."

"The Protector" is a monument to (then) modern technology. Long before engines and turbines were even dreamed of, man-power was the dynamo that got this huge fire apparatus from the station to the fire.

"It is interesting that these huge pumper units continued on in use after newer trucks came along. They were used for musters, reunions, parades, and competitions. The hand-pump competitions were exciting. A bunch of these old fire wagons would gather from all over New England, and they would hold all kinds of competitions. The high point was the water shoot. They would line these magnificent old beasts up, and at the given signal, all of the assembled men would run to their hand-pumper and get to work. They pumped mightily, and eventually the water came blasting out of the main hose. It was hard work, and so the departments would send their strongest men to the contests. It must have been something to see," Galligan told me.

On display is a large judge's ledger from one of these competitions. It was the 44th New England Muster held on July 20, 1935, and various fire departments sent their old hand-pumpers for the contest. Brockton's "Protector" had a decent showing on this day but it was no match for the ultimate winner, "The Vixen" from Berwick, Maine, which shot a stream of water a whopping 167 feet.

"And all of that with manpower," Galligan said softly as he shook his head.

I remarked on the great condition of a lot of the items on display at the museum.

"Well, we were lucky," Galligan began. "A lot of this stuff was earmarked for destruction. Nobody wanted any of it. For example, this fire call center. We literally saved this from being thrown in a trash compactor by about twelve hours. And look at this marvelous item."

The entire fire call system of the city of Brockton was being thrown out to be upgraded. Galligan and his friends got wind of this, raced to the firehouse, packed it all up, and took it to storage before the sledge hammers could do their damage. The center is an astonishing piece of history. It is literally the complete workings of a fire call system that was standard in Brockton for more than fifty years. And it is all in good working condition.

"Here, pretend you are calling in a fire," he instructed. "Go ahead, pull the lever."

I opened the old corner call box door and pulled the lever. With that it set everything in front of me in motion. A bell rang on the wall alerting the entire city's station that an address was coming in. Then a long white tape unspooled in front of me, punching out the holes indicating which street and which house was on fire. Levers clicked, bells rang, lights blinked. It was quite exciting to watch. And it was efficient.

"At the sound of the first bell all of the lights automatically went on in the firehouse that was to respond. Later, it also shut off the electricity to that firehouse."

Why would it do that?

"In case the firemen were cooking on a stove and ran out and forget their meal was still there. This prevented them from coming back to a fire at their own station," the old chief said with a grin.

Wow Factor

"That would be over in the corner," Carl Landerholm said. He is the president of the Brockton Historical Society and joined us for our tour.

In the corner is the story of one of the worst fire department tragedies in American history.

"On March 10, 1941, our giant downtown movie theater caught fire. It was bad, and a number of our firemen were killed when the burning roof of the theater collapsed and sent them into the inferno. Twelve died that night, and one died the next day. It was the single largest fire department loss until September 11, 2001. As you can imagine, the city was rocked by it," Landerholm told me.

The Brockton Fire Memorial display features newspaper clippings, memorabilia, photographs, and a somber, larger-than-life statue of a grieving Brockton fireman with his head bowed.

"Here is the list of those who died," he said as he pointed to a wall plaque. I read the names. Kelly, O'Brien, McKeraghan, Sullivan, Murphy, McGeary.

"Some say you had to be Irish if you were in the fire department," he reflected. "Such a tragedy. All good lads."

The Takeaway

This is one of the most impressive fire museums I have been to. While the fire vehicles are pretty old, they tell the dramatic story of a different time, a more difficult time in the history of American firefighting. It clearly illustrates how bone-weary these firemen must have been after answering a call. The displays are wonderful, and the operation of the entire old fire call center is a real show-stopper.

The Nuts and Bolts

Brockton Fire Museum

216 North Pearl Street
Brockton, Massachusetts 02301
(508) 583-0039
www.brocktonhistoricalsociety.org
This museum is handicapped accessible.

Travel Suggestion

The Brockton Historical Society, including the fire museum, is located at a very busy three-corner intersection, so keep your eye out for it or you will miss it as you try and navigate the tricky traffic pattern.

Museum Hours

The museum is open every first and third Sunday of the month or by appointment.

Admission

Adults: $2.00
Children under 12: Free

Up around the Bend

After finishing your visit to the fire museum, stroll over to the main historical society building (located in the same museum complex). Here are two other small museums worth your time. The Brockton Shoe Museum tells the story of the shoe industry in the city. Brockton once made more shoes here than anywhere else in the world. Also, there is the Rocky Marciano Museum. Marciano, a one-time world heavyweight boxing champion, was a native of the city, and there is a small area here where you can see the "Brockton Blockbuster's" bronzed boxing gloves, historical memorabilia, and archival videos.

20 Museum of Antiquated Technology

⸻

Hanson

It appears as if Mark Vess has never thrown anything away. Ever.

"Sure, it gets a little crowded in here, but these rooms are my world. I just love it in here," he said. "Here" is two floors of a large carriage house attached to his beautiful home in Hanson. He refers to these two rooms as the "Museum of Antiquated Technology."

"I have had an interest in everything electrical since I was a kid. In fact, my father was an engineer. I started collecting gadgets when I was very young, and I followed that interest into a long-time career as a research and development specialist for a major biomedical company. Now I am retired, so I can go back to being a kid again," he said.

Vess's vast collection, now numbering well into the thousands of pieces, covers every inch of the floors, walls, and even ceilings of this large, barn-like structure.

"The ground floor I call the Workshop. Visitors who really love engineering, electrical oddities, and just the whole notion of how things work like it in here. I am a licensed ham radio operator (KC1-ACF) so I have several radios to tinker with." At this he picked up a microphone, did a call-out, and within seconds was chatting away with a far-off airwaves friend. Many of Vess's items are valuable originals dating back to the halcyon days of big, boxy, elaborate early radio transmitters and receivers. His pride and joy is a 1923 Atwater Kent radio. Of course, it is in perfect working condition.

"These old tube varieties were monstrosities, but when the transistor came along in the late 1940s, that is when things really started to get interesting. He showed me a table with a collection of vintage transistor AM radios that would melt the heart of any baby boomer worth his (or her) salt.

"Come on, Chuck, which one did you have?" he asked. I looked them over, and there it was. A small, fire engine red 1962 Channel Master Six transistor radio, with a chrome front and a metal flip-out table-stand on the back. "That one right there," I said with glee. "I remember listening to WBZ in Boston late at night all the way from rural central New York when I was a kid in the 1950s," I told him as I caressed this nostalgic bridge to my past.

He winked and gave me a knowing smile.

"Let's go up to the museum," he said.

The second floor of Vess's carriage barn is as equally packed with memorabilia as the first. But with a different spin to it all.

"This is my collection; this is my life," he said as he switched on the light.

In front of me were thousands of items he has collected over more than six decades. Most impressive was a wall of old cabinet radios, with their wooden cases still gleaming in the afternoon sun streaming in from the windows.

"We span forty years of radios back here. I have several Crosley radios. They were pioneers and are highly collectible. They were the Model T Ford of the tube radio industry. They made millions of them. In fact their motto was, 'For every man, a Crossley.'

"Here is a rare one," he continued, as we gingerly tiptoed over an assortment of items jumbled on the floor. "It is the oldest one that I have. It is a 1913 Murdock, very similar to Marconi's original radio. It is very rare, and I love it. It works and is a marvel of electrical genius. There was only one problem," he said.

"What?"

"There were no radio stations yet," he exclaimed.

This mini-Smithsonian is either a hit or miss with the visitors that make their way to Vess's house.

"Some stay for ten minutes," he told me. "Others stay for a whole day. And then come back the next day."

A whole shelf is filled with vintage 16mm movie projectors. Among the other items on display are hundreds of electrical gadgets, dozens of straight razors, and an area filled with old Victrolas and 1950s television sets. A table with rows of old flashlights, toasters, waffle irons, cameras, clocks, and too many other items to count.

"With a little nudge I can get almost every single item in here to work," he noted.

I asked Vess if out of this scrum of technological bric-a-brac he could find a favorite item?

"Sure. It is this thing right here. They don't use them anymore of course. But this is the first item I ever collected. It was my dad's, and he gave it to me when I was a boy. I cherish it," he said as he cradled the odd looking item.

It was a slide rule.

Wow Factor

"I love medical quackery," the owner told me. "The more bizarre, the stranger it gets, the more I like it. And this one takes the cake."

Vess took me to a corner of the room and pulled out an elaborate box. The red label said "Master Violet Ray." Sounds a little creepy, I commented.

"Oh, this is wonderful. It is from 1925, and medical quacks sold them to people as a way of curing what ails you." He took the item out. It is a long, glass tube with a flat-footed end. When the switch is thrown, this handheld device comes alive with a stream of white glowing rarefied gas inside the main tube and a purple emission coming out of the end. He waved it over my palm and it gave off a crackling sensation as electricity arced from the device through the air to my skin.

"People would have these in their homes and use them when they felt ill. They would simply wave this glass wand over the place that was bothering them, and then they would be cured. The list of ailments that it said it could fix was virtually endless, from cramps to headaches to sore feet to diarrhea. People bought these items like they were going out of style."

I asked Vess if he trusted this item to do what it promised to do.

"Of course not," he laughed. "It was quackery at its finest, and that is why it is my wow factor."

The Takeaway

One of the most important pieces of advice I give people who explore the topics of my museum books is to ask. Ask. If you don't, the contents of a museum just stare blankly back at you, leaving you to wonder what the untold story is. Ask. There is no problem in asking at the Museum of Antiquated Technology; this is in Mark Vess's private residence, and you are sure to get a personal tour of the museum each and every time. And that makes a major difference, especially in a place as specific as this.

Vess is an elfin figure, with pink cheeks and white mutton chops ringing his lively face. He is the perfect guide to this unique and interesting museum.

The Nuts and Bolts

Museum of Antiquated Technology

303 High Street
Hanson, Massachusetts 02341
(781) 294-1647
www.antiquatedtech.weebly.com
This museum is not handicapped accessible.

Travel Suggestion

Vess's home is in a residential area with no sign out front. Your landmark is Hanson's community water tower across the street from his house.

Museum Hours

Vess welcomes visitors anytime to tour his museum. However, since this is a private residence, you must call in advance for an appointment. For information about a tour, you can call Vess or email him at vessmuseumtech@aol.com.

Admission

Free

Up around the Bend

Pembroke, Massachusetts, is just four miles east of Hanson. This historic little New England town has several interesting historic landmarks to explore. A popular one is the Pembroke Friends Meetinghouse. Built in 1706, it is one of the oldest Quaker sites in America. The interior is divided in two: women sat on one side of the building, men on the other.

21 Beer Can Museum

~~~⌒~~~

East Taunton

Museums come in all shapes and sizes, and they can focus on any number of subjects. There are large art museums and smaller local history museums. Some museums are made up of a single person's private collection. That is the case with the Beer Can Museum.

It is the ultimate man cave.

"I have over five thousand beer cans on display, from over sixty different countries," said Kevin Logan, owner and curator of the Beer Can Museum. "I like them for their artistic beauty, but of course many of these can become quite valuable. Still, they are really little miniature works of art. With beer inside. It's perfect."

The museum completely fills the large basement of Logan's private residence. At the foot of the cellar stairs he will run an eight-minute video to tease you for what is to come. The beer

cans begin right at the landing of the steps and continue in cases, on tables, on the walls, on the ceilings, and dangling from every inch of this extra-large basement. Lit beer signs twinkle and add a festive, carnival atmosphere to the whole place.

I asked him how it all started.

"Well, I still have the first beer can that I collected. It was 1978, I was just fourteen years old, and I was in Galveston with my family. I came upon a can of Falstaff beer and next I got a can each of Lone Star and Texas Pride. That was the foundation for the five thousand cans that followed," he said. He still has those three first cans in his basement.

The display is positively dizzying. I scanned the labels and names on some of the cans, most of which I had never heard of before: Dallas Blonde, Simpler Times Lager, Fox DeLuxe, Star Banner Ale, Frankenmuth Melody, and others.

"What part of the world do you come from, Chuck" he asked me. When I told him I had deep roots in central New York, he quickly picked out cans that immediately brought me back to my college years. Utica Club, Schaeffer, Matts, Genesee, and a couple of beers from my college town of Albany were easily found by the curator.

"That is what I like to do. When folks stop by, they are amazed at how quickly I can locate a beer from their past and from their hometown area. I don't think I have ever been stumped."

Beers are loosely arranged by themes. There are lots of pop culture cans, featuring everything from the likes of the infamous Billy (Carter) Beer, to J. R. (Ewing) Beer, to Mickey Gilley's Beer, to M*A*S*H Beer from the old television show.

"Sports are very big, and I eventually had to stop collecting them. NASCAR, NFL, baseball. They are all big. Teams especially in our Boston area are always coming out with something new, and I just don't have the room to keep up with them. And besides, the vintage ones are my favorites anyways."

A very large and especially attractive section features beer cans from around the world. "I have my spotters who will find a lot of these. The international beer cans are strikingly beautiful, and they are some of the best, as far as art goes." On display are cans from the Dominican Republic and other parts of the Caribbean, Israel, Switzerland, Russia, Japan, and Africa. The most unusual one was a beer from Tunisia, with a label in Arabic.

"It is interesting to me because this beautiful can came from a Muslim country where, presumably, nobody is supposed to drink beer," he told me.

Logan even features an area of beer cans with sexy and X-rated labels. Most of them are international. "I do ask for I.D. if someone wants to see that section," he said.

All of these cans are empty although you would never know it. Kevin flipped a can over. "We beer can collectors open up the cans from the bottom so they are more attractively displayed." Sure enough, the scars of an old church key were visible on the bottom of every can.

Logan is a real source authority for beer-can aficionados around the world. "I get calls and letters all the time asking me how much a certain can is worth, or wanting a quote about the art of beer-can collecting." He showed me a letter he recently received from the History Channel asking about the most expensive beer can ever sold. "I was able to tell them that a can once sold for $18,000. I get a lot of that. Verification inquiries."

So, I asked him. Where is that $18,000 beer can?

He peered over his glasses and said, "I wish."

Wow Factor

"As I said, I get great enjoyment watching visitors find that one beer can that really takes them back to their younger days, or one that really touches a memory for them. It is mostly the guys, but some females do this also. But my wow factor would have to be this."

Kevin showed me a faded old color photograph on the wall. In it are five shirtless GI's sweltering in a tent in Chu-Lai, Vietnam. They are smiling at the camera and have their arms around each other. Clearly, these were buddies far from home in a difficult situation. "I got a letter from one of the soldiers asking me to try and identify the beer that they were drinking in the photograph."

The picture shows just the top of a can in the front lower left of the photographs. These guys, who survived the war, obviously have an affinity for that beer from so long ago. There is not much to see of the can.

"I knew in an instant," Logan told me. "In fact I have the cans right here. They were drinking Hamm's beer, circa 1968. They probably got it at a makeshift PX in the jungles of Vietnam. I contacted the soldier who wrote to me. He was thrilled. Funny how things mean so much to people. It was a great honor to help them out. It was touching to be a part of such an unusual and yet poignant memory for these guys."

The Takeaway

As the above story illustrates, there is a connection between us older guys and the beer we drank when we were kids in college, out of high school, or in the service. I felt it personally when he handed me a 1960s-era can of Genny Cream Ale. It took me back to my own college days when I was living in Albany, New York, going to classes and trying to scrape together eighty-nine cents to buy a six-pack of the beer to enjoy on a weekend with my friends. Logan doesn't only deal with memories at his museum. He instructs on the various trends, brewing techniques, changing tastes, and historic lore and legends of the beer industry in America. He knows his stuff, and although he does not call himself an expert on the beverage ("I am a beer *can* expert. Not a *beer* expert"), you can see why so many organizations through the years have turned to him for advice and information.

I liked the quirkiness of the museum. There was a surprise on every shelf. Kind of a collection of "mini wow factors." A replicated Budweiser can called "Bodmaicer" that was yanked out of the refrigerator by Al Bundy in virtually every episode of *Married with Children*. A German beer can that doubles as a music box. And, perhaps the oddest one I found, a can of beer that can actually track sharks. It came from Nantucket and had a scanning chip on the can to tell you where sharks were.

I felt a kinship to this museum. I guess we all hope that there is a place like this and a person like Logan to act as the keeper of our beer memories.

As I left, I had to ask, "What on earth does your wife think about all of this?"

"Well, let me just say that my wife is a saint," he replied. "And she doesn't drink beer."

The Nuts and Bolts

Beer Can Museum

1039-A Middleboro Avenue
East Taunton, Massachusetts 02718
No phone. (See below for contact information.)
http://kevslog.tripod.com/beercanmuseum
This museum is not handicapped accessible.

Travel Suggestion

The museum is located in a residential area and there is
no sign out front.

Museum Hours

The museum is open by appointment only. For information, visit the museum's website or email Kevin Logan at
beercanmuseum@gmail.com.

Admission

Free

Up around the Bend

Nearby Taunton has one of Massachusetts's most famous village
greens. For over a century the community has decorated it elaborately for Christmas, and thousands come to witness the holiday
spectacle annually. This has led Taunton to adopt as its nickname
"The Christmas City."

22 Dighton Rock Museum

Berkley

This is perhaps the most unusual museum in this book.

The Dighton Rock Museum is located along the Taunton River at the edge of a state park. A small, white building holds "the rock," and when it is open, visitors are able to stroll inside to see it and learn what it actually is.

What it actually is is, well, a rock. A giant, forty-ton boulder that ended a ten thousand–year meandering journey here some fifty miles south of Boston. The thing that makes this rock so unusual, so unique, so mysterious is the set of carvings found covering its face. Experts have been studying this rock for many years, especially since it was dragged out of the riverbed and housed in its own little museum for the entire world to see in 1963.

Inside the little museum (which is unattended), visitors can study panels that put forth several of the theories behind these ancient rock carvings. Some say they were etched into the stone by American Indians, the Phoenicians, Norse Vikings, or more recently the Portuguese. Not knowing where this thousands-of-years-old rock began its tumble to Berkley, some have even suggested that the Chinese are responsible for its present artistic condition. The palette for the carvings is a five-feet high, ten-feet wide, eleven-feet deep chunk of crystalline sandstone. The carvings are dramatically lit so they are easy to view.

To decipher the meaning of the markings (called petroglyphs), one would have to be well-versed in the deep nuances of several ancient cultures. Some of the images are of long lost coats of arms, numeric characters, crude maps, or perhaps even royal charters. There are even a variety of religious icons. It is impossible to tell the exact age of the carvings or what carving instruments were used. Some of the mysterious images are etched in a series nearly ten feet long and a foot and a half broad.

For many years the boulder lay in the water, partially uncovered by the whims of the tides. Eventually interest became so great that it was lifted from its silty bed and placed forever more in this tiny museum.

It remains a Massachusetts enigma.

Wow Factor

Since this is an unattended museum whose doors are opened by appointment only or when park staff is on the grounds, visitors will take from a stop here their own personal wow factors. The rock in and of itself is a fascinating story. But I found that the backstory of the concerned local citizenry "rescuing" it from the muck of the river bottom and placing it in its own shrine very inspirational.

The Takeaway

The good people of Berkley and Dighton are to be applauded for their great care and interest in the preservation of Dighton Rock. The park that now surrounds the museum is beautiful and well-tended. Picnic tables and outdoor grilling areas abound. Restrooms are available, and the ground is flat and easily accessible for those in wheelchairs.

In 1963, the rock was lifted from the water and placed on dry land surrounded by a tall chain-link fence. In 1973, this oddity was attracting more and more attention, by casual visitors and experts alike, and the rock was housed in a glass-enclosed building. A year later, a museum dedicated to the Dighton Rock was authorized by the Massachusetts legislature (House Bill 5475). Now an official Massachusetts State Park consisting of more than eighty acres, the whole area is a pleasant diversion along the road less traveled. In 1980, the rock was listed on the National Register of Historic Places.

The Dighton Rock Museum sits directly on the water's edge, and from the back ledge one can see the peaceful, reedy shores of the river stretching out on both sides. Visitors can view some beautiful homes across the water and watch expensive yachts slipping in and out of the Taunton Yacht Club directly opposite the museum. The museum river site is a center for bird watching as more than 150 species have been seen along the shores including kingfishers, osprey, heron, and bald eagles.

The park is a venue for many public events including Native

American cultural and music programs, landscape painting workshops, archaeological seminars, and instructional programs, some of them conducted by Harvard University, which focus on the history and mystery of Dighton Rock itself.

The Nuts and Bolts

Dighton Rock Museum

Dighton Rock State Park
Third Avenue
Berkley, Massachusetts 02779
(508) 822-7537 or (508) 644-5522
www.mass.gov/locations/dighton-rock-state-park
This is an unstaffed museum in a public park.
It is wheelchair accessible.

Travel Suggestion

Dighton Rock State Park is in a very sparsely populated area. Keep your eyes open for the park sign on your right as you travel south from the town of Berkley about three miles.

Museum Hours

The museum is open by appointment only for individual or group visits. Park attendants will also open the museum if they are working on the grounds during your visit. For museum information or event schedules, call the museum or visit the Friends of Dighton Rock Facebook page at https://www.facebook.com/Friends OfDightonRockMuseum.

Admission

Free

Up around the Bend

Rehoboth is a quaint Massachusetts village just ten miles west of Berkley. It is one of the state's oldest communities (1643). Rehoboth has several historic mid-1700s buildings and a whopping fifty-three cemeteries to explore.

REGION FOUR
Cape Cod

23 Coast Guard Heritage Museum

Barnstable

There are many historic buildings on Cape Cod. This museum in Barnstable is among the most striking. It is a proud two-story red brick former U.S. Custom House and post office. It has tall, curved arch windows and sits on a grassy knoll from where in its original days it could see the Barnstable Harbor. On the grounds of this museum you will also find a working village smithy, which presents blacksmithing demonstrations, as well as a Barnstable jail known as "The Oldest Wooden Jail in America."

"But, this is *not* the U.S. Coast Guard Museum," Captain H. F. "Buck" Baley reminded me. A longtime Coast Guard veteran and board member of the museum, Baley told me why there is confusion on this issue. "Well, the official U.S. Coast Guard Museum is in the works and will be located in New London, Connecticut. Our museum is the Coast Guard Heritage Museum. We are not operated by the Coast Guard but rather by a group of retired personnel from the service, local historians, and others who are interested in military preservation. We opened our doors in May 2005. We do not own this magnificent building, but rather we lease it from the town of Barnstable."

Inside the front door of the museum visitors are welcomed by soaring ceilings, high windows, large display cases filled with maritime memorabilia, and enough scale model ships to send any young (or old) model maker into a trance.

"This building itself is quite unusual. It actually is an early pre-fabricated structure. It came to here in pieces and was put together on this spot. It was a metal building that was then encased in red brick. Never quite knowing what the building was destined for, it came with an array of unusual features."

Baley pointed to the large staircase leading to the second floor. "You see a large metal door right there in the middle of the stairs? The door leads to nothing. Open it and you will be in midair. Still, it was part of the design so that is the way it arrived. We have our very own 'door to nowhere.'" Another intriguing feature is the heating system. "These tall fluted columns, which appear to be holding the ceiling up, are merely there to disguise the heating ducts inside them. Surprisingly, the heat came out of the top and not the bottom."

Other parts of the interior show the echoes of its duty as a post office. "You can still see the dip in the old oak floors where the mail clerks stood over the years servicing thousands of customers waiting to mail a letter." The dip, located in front of old frosted-glass service windows marked "Registry" and "Money Orders," is very noticeable.

"Our museum strives to trace the timeline of the U.S. Coast Guard from its earliest days as the U.S. Revenue Cutter Service, which collected the revenue from incoming ships, through its merger and with the U.S. Lifesaving Service, which itself basically emerged from a volunteer group who positioned themselves along the coast helping out in times of maritime distress as part of the Massachusetts Humane Society. The final merger into the U.S. Coast Guard happened in 1915."

Every inch of the museum is filled with uniforms, photographs, old weapons, paintings, vintage sailing equipment, newspaper clippings, and more that covers the entire history of the Coast Guard up to modern times. And lots of model ships.

"We were very fortunate to have a number of the premier ship model makers in the country involved in this museum. One in particular, Mike Maynard, a retired Coast Guard cook, has loaned many of his Smithsonian-quality Coast Guard ship models for us to display. They are always a highlight of a visit to this museum."

Maynard's models defy description. The subjects are ships from all different Coast Guard eras. The largest model, which is one of the first things a visitor sees upon entering the museum, is a giant scale model of the current USCG Cutter *Campbell*. The *Campbell* is a 270-foot medium endurance cutter. The model maker has captured the ship in such fine detail that a visitor discovers something new about it with every viewing. The scale model highlights all of the work stations on the ship, all the equipment, rigging, identification marks, decks, and more. There are dozens of tiny officers and guardsmen going about their daily routine on the high seas. One humorous vignette is played out near the stern of the ship. Here we see miniscule models of an officer chewing out a sailor who has spilled a pail of paint on the deck.

"This is our pride and joy," Baley said as we peered through glass at this large model. "Look," he pointed. "He even painted some rust stains on the side of the ship."

Wow Factor

"We have a display exhibit of items pertaining to the USCG Lifeboat *36500*. Although this boat, its crew, and its exploits have been well known in the Coast Guard family for decades, it has been only recently that its story has been presented to the general public. On February 18, 1952, the crew of the *36500* set out in a fierce storm to rescue the crew of a disabled oil tanker, the SS *Pendleton*. Legend and lore now describe the rescue of thirty-two of the thirty-three *Pendleton* crewmembers as virtually miraculous. The story was told in a 2009 book which was later made into the Hollywood movie *The Finest Hours*. The tanker, broken in half in a terrible storm, was adrift in the sea off the coast of Chatham. A crew of just four overcame every imaginable obstacle to go out there, get those guys, and return safely. One of those heroic crewmen was Boatswain's Mate First Class Bernard Webber. As you can see, our exhibit includes personal items of his as well as Webber family memorabilia.

"The *36500* was quite a boat. And she is still afloat. She is owned by the Orleans Historical Society, just a few miles from the museum."

The Takeaway

The museum staff is made up entirely by volunteers. Buck Baley was an excellent tour guide, and his many years of service in the

USCG give him excellent credibility when he spins tales about the service and describes the multitude of items on display here. His passion for the Coast Guard is palpable and sincere. During one portion of our tour we came to a long line of USCG uniforms. They showed the subtle design changes over the decades, and Baley pointed them all out to me. And subtle is the key word. "Years of tradition unhampered by progress," he told me. As we left, he turned and said, "Here is an interesting one, Chuck." He tugged on the sleeve of a formal dress uniform. "Recognize the name tag?" he asked. I looked closely at the name on the chest.

"Baley."

One room on the second floor is dedicated to the U.S. Lighthouse Service and is also very interesting. Again, there are some superb scale models of the historic lightships that plied the choppy Atlantic waters not far from where we were standing. The remainder of the second floor includes displays on small boat operations, the Coast Guard at war, and Coast Guard aviation.

Buck Baley kept referring to the men and women in the USCG as family. "Coasties are all members of the same family," he said. There was one special item that brought this all together for me.

"This is the large ship's bell from the Coast Guard Cutter *White Sage*," he explained. The bell was indeed large, polished to a dazzling, reflective silver, and hanging from a thick ship's rope. "Run your hand up and inside the bell," he directed me.

I felt the smooth curves of the unseen inside of the bell but my hand was interrupted several times by something protruding from the sides of the bell's interior.

"Come down here and look inside," he said. I did. Inside the bell, attached to the sides were little personal plaques, each with a name and a date.

"The ship was commissioned in September 1947 and decommissioned in 1996. During that time, whenever a crew member became a new father, the ship's bell was taken down, overturned, and used as the actual baptismal font for the new baby. Those names in there are the names of the new infants."

Baley was right. Family.

The Nuts and Bolts

Coast Guard Heritage Museum

3353 Main Street
Barnstable, Massachusetts 02630
(508) 362-8521
www.coastguardheritagemuseum.org
The main floor is handicapped accessible.

Travel Suggestion

The museum is located two blocks east of the
Barnstable County Courthouse complex in
Barnstable Village. Main Street is Route 6A,
also known as "The Old King's Highway."

Museum Hours

May through October: Tuesday to Saturday, 10 a.m.
to 3 p.m.

Admission

Adults: $5.00
Children (under 10) and active-duty USCG members:
Free

Up around the Bend

The Orleans Historical Society, caretakers of the famous USCG 36500, is located twenty miles east of Barnstable. For information, visit http://www.orleanshistoricalsociety.org.

US CAPE COD HYANNIS Statue of John F. Kennedy at the JFK Museum by
Gerrit de Heus/Alamy Stock Photo.

24 John F. Kennedy Hyannis Museum

Hyannis

There are three museums in Massachusetts that are dedicated to the life and times of native son and the thirty-fifth president of the United States, John Fitzgerald Kennedy.

One, in Boston, is an imposing white concrete edifice surrounded by glass windows. The museum tower, which is 125 feet tall, offers a stunning water view that includes the skyline of Boston in the distance. A massive wall of windows welcomes sunlight into the confines of the structure adding to the sense of being outdoors at the museum. The building has two theaters, many artifacts and collections, and is, of course, the official home of the John F. Kennedy Presidential Library. The building was designed by architect I. M. Pei. Tens of thousands of people from all over the world visit here each year.

A second one is the late president's birthplace in Brookline. It is credentialed as a National Historic Site and is run under the auspices of the National Park Service.

This is the third one.

"Our museum is obviously much different than the Boston sites. Our lens is on John F. Kennedy and his family here on Cape Cod. We are not a presidential library," John Allen, the museum's executive director, said. "Our museum was formed in 1992 as a result of so many tourists and visitors to Hyannis asking, 'where is the Kennedy compound?' Well, the compound is located here, but it is strictly private and can really only be viewed from the water. So we wanted to give visitors an outlet to explore the Kennedy story while they were here. After all, the name Kennedy is synonymous with Cape Cod. Visitors want to see and feel his presence, his legacy. This has become a worldwide destination for many. In fact, 22 percent of our visitors come from outside the United States. Kennedy was beloved by people around the world."

This small, red brick museum, located in the 1926 former Hyannis Town Hall, sees a steady stream of people coming through. On the day I visited, they included a small school group, a senior citizen charter bus group, some young couples with babies on their backs, and a few scholars who were researching the Kennedy administration.

"Yes, it is a wonderful mix of young and old alike here," Allen observed. "They come here to see the images, and we have hundreds. They want to relive, if only for a moment, Camelot and a different time and era that JFK represented. He gave people hope, vision, and inspiration. Take the space race for example. He told us we could land a man on the moon, we believed him, and he delivered. That is what people come here for."

The museum photographs, which center on the president's life in Hyannis, are voluminous and well displayed. We see Kennedy at work and at play, before, during, and after elections, as well as visiting with his neighbors and sailing off the shore of Cape Cod. A separate exhibit, which covers an entire room, is dedicated to the president's mother, Rose Kennedy, who lived to be 104. Unlike the busyness of the much larger museum in Boston, this space is perfect for those who want to take their time going through it, those who want an unhurried and personal experience. Each photograph is worth a few minutes. They are all clearly captioned and focus on a different aspect of JFK's home life.

"People are amazed at both the number of the photographs here and the sheer scope of their content. We have photographs that you will only see in this museum. In fact, Ethel Kennedy [Robert Kennedy's widow] stopped by recently, and she remarked that she saw pictures displayed here that even she had never seen before."

Wow Factor

"Obviously, President Kennedy's assassination was a seminal moment in so many of our lives, in the life of our country even. But here JFK is always forty-six years old. We know he was forty-six at the time of his death, but he lives on here forever young. Still, we must recognize what happened on November 22, 1963, in this museum, and we do. My wow factor is what I call the 'dark panel.'"

The panel is a single, large photograph at the end of a long line of "timeline photos." It is fitting that it comes at the end of a series of presidential photos. It is clear this is the picture that signifies the end of an era.

"This photo, taken by White House photographer Jacques Lowe, would go on to become one of the most famous presidential photos ever taken. It shows President Kennedy and his brother Robert. They are silhouetted against a backdrop of the

White House. They are both in deep thought. Knowing what we now know, that the president would be murdered and that, a short time later, his brother would meet the same fate, is just so poignant to me and to everybody who views it. It shows the continuum of the Kennedy family. They carry on. They always have. They have met tragedy, many tragedies, but they keep going. People can relate to that."

As we stood in front of this "dark panel," I could sense that Allen was getting emotional. I asked him why he had such a strong connection to the president and to this museum.

"When I was a young man, John Kennedy inspired me. He still does. He was our president at a changing time, an exciting time. He was so young and so bright. He had a beautiful wife and two little children. He made changes. Changes in the office that people could see. Arts and culture came back to the White House. He was the first president to institute Air Force One as the official presidential plane. The Peace Corps. Special Olympics. It just goes on and on. It was hope and energy and love and devotion. We still see that today. When John F. Kennedy, Jr., died in a plane crash near here in 1999, people were stunned. Another Kennedy tragedy. John Jr. was only thirty-eight. People needed a place to express their sadness. We opened our doors that weekend, and ten thousand people came through our museum doors. That is almost the whole population of Hyannis. We were here for them."

"Here, let me show you something, Chuck," he said to me. We were standing in front of the dark panel. He reached deep into his front pants pocket. He pulled out a coin. "I have carried one of these with me for over forty years," he said as he fingered the silver coin. "It helps me remember. I was just a kid in college when he was killed, but his spirit moved me. And that feeling is with me to this day."

I asked him if I could see the coin. He handed it to me. It was a Kennedy half-dollar.

The Takeaway

Presidential history and memorabilia are right up this author's alley. I am the same age as John Allen and have the same reflective feeling about JFK as he did. I have been to the library and museum in Boston. This one in Hyannis is a must-see for visitors to Cape Cod and for those who also have been inspired by our former president.

While the photographs are the bulk of the museum, and they are fascinating, there is a lot of memorabilia of Kennedy and his family here as well. A home movie of him sailing in the waters off the Cape and then frolicking at home with his kids at the compound plays nonstop.

The museum is very much a living museum, and it stays connected to its host community in various ways. They hold interesting speakers every year as well as book signings, author talks, receptions, and video screenings. One ongoing project is a video-sharing project with schools across the country that are named after President Kennedy.

"Oh, it is so interesting! We contact the school and organize a Facebook video gathering between the museum and the students. It is always lively and fun and lets us get our word out. In fact, we just recently did our one hundredth school. It was the John F. Kennedy Elementary School in Great Neck, Long Island. Five hundred kids! Wow. We had a wonderful time with them."

The Nuts and Bolts

John F. Kennedy Hyannis Museum

397 Main Street
Hyannis, Massachusetts 02601
(508) 790-3077
www.jfkhyannismuseum.org
This museum is handicapped accessible.

Travel Suggestion

The museum is literally in the heart of the downtown
business district of Hyannis. A life-sized bronze statue of
President Kennedy stands in front of the entrance.

Museum Hours

April 13 through May 31: Monday to Saturday, 10 a.m.
to 4 p.m.; Sunday, 12 p.m. to 4 p.m.
June 1 through October 31: Monday to Saturday, 9 a.m.
to 5 p.m.; Sunday, 12 p.m. to 5 p.m.
November 1 through November 29: Monday to Saturday,
10 a.m. to 4 p.m.; Sunday, 12 p.m. to 4 p.m.
Closed December 1 through mid-April, except school
vacation week

Admission

Adults: $12.00
Children (6–17) and students with ID: $6.00
Seniors (62+): $10.00
Private tours can be scheduled while the museum is
closed. Please call Jennifer Pappalardo at
(508) 790-3077, ext. 3, to discuss your visit in detail.

Up around the Bend

After you visit the museum, take a short, four-block drive to Veterans Memorial Park and see the Kennedy Memorial. The harbor views are spectacular, and the memorial, which features a large image of the president, is a fitting tribute from those who knew him best. The setting is beautiful.

Photograph by John Phelan. Creative Commons license available at:
https://creativecommons.org/licenses/by/3.0/.

25 French Cable Station Museum

⌒∽

Orleans

This little white Cape-style house on a side street in Orleans looks like it came from the set of *Mayberry, R.F.D.* or even *Father Knows Best*. It is understated, New England–plain, and anonymous in every way.

But, oh what a story this little white house can tell. The inside of this home was an eyewitness to one of the great engineering marvels of the nineteenth century.

In the early to mid-1850s, the United States was investing heavily in the laying of undersea communication cables to Europe. By 1854, telegraph wires had been strung over 23,000 miles in the United States. This made slow yet reliable transmission of messages within our borders one of the most remarkable achievements of the era. But to get a message to Europe was arduous, unreliable, expensive, and basically impossible. A message that needed to be delivered from, say, Philadelphia to Paris in 1860 involved a one-month turnaround trip by ship. Still, Cyrus Field of Stockbridge, Massachusetts, was not deterred easily.

With dogged determination, he signed on seaworthy crews, took control of two giant ships to lay the cable, and set forth with a plan to snake a transmission cable from one continent to another. Several times weather intervened in the worst way. On numerous other occasions the cable was successfully dropped to the sea floor only to have it break. Bringing the cable to the surface to splice it together was difficult and time-consuming work. But he prevailed.

On August 16, 1858, another transoceanic message, this one transmitted underwater by Field's cable, was sent from Queen Victoria to President Buchanan. This message ushered in one of the great advances in world communication. Our president called the event "a triumph more glorious . . . than was ever won by a conqueror on the field of battle." Historians have called this feat the "Moon Shot of the Nineteenth Century."

It took sixteen hours for the message to make its way across the floor of the North Atlantic Ocean, some 2,500 miles. But high costs and bad weather hampered the cable's output, and ultimately transmission times slowed to a snail's pace. Three weeks after the exchange of salutations between the United States and England, the cable was closed.

"This house was a part of one of history's greatest achievements. You'd never know by looking at it would you," said Lucien Ozon, vice president of the French Cable Museum. "This house was built by the French Cable Company in 1891 and was used to receive and send message to France. The cable came up right behind this house in the cove. The house was filled with electronic equipment, very sophisticated for its time. Twenty-four people manned the property all day, every day. They got the messages and then resent them to all over the United States. Because we had to send to California, they had to have people in here at night. My father worked here as a telegraph operator. He came from the area of Saint Pierre and Miquelon, territories of France in Newfoundland, Canada. The majority of the messages sent and received in here were for the financial markets, such as Wall Street. The cable between America and France originally stretched from Europe to a remote section on the far eastern end of Cape Cod. Winters were brutal at that location so they moved the station into the commercial section of Orleans for better operational conditions. This house was owned by France and was an active entity until it was closed on Thanksgiving Day, 1959."

Ozon's patois is heavy and thick with the French nuances of Atlantic Canada. His face is weathered and voice raspy, but his mind is clear. He is eighty years old. "I remember this place so well," he said. "Always busy, always exciting. In those days Cape Cod was nothing but a barren sand dune. No tourists, no hotels, no McDonalds," he laughed. "But this job, the work my father did here, was specialized. It was serious. Not everybody could do it. It was one of the highest paying jobs you could get on the Cape. They called it a 'New York salary.' The workers had benefits, a union, and were treated like professionals. My father was a high-roller. He bought a new car every year. The pay was good because of our location. It was so remote out here that the company actually paid the men 'hardship wages,'" he told me.

Joseph Manas is the president of the French Cable Museum. "This little house has been here for decades. A lot of people never knew what went on here, what the importance was of what they did here, until we turned it into a museum. The French cable was known as 'Le Direct,' and it went from Orleans, Massachusetts, to Brest, France, a distance of 3,173 miles. It lasted from 1898 to 1959. It was deemed so important that U.S. Marines guarded this little house during wartime. In World War I, General Pershing communicated with, and got his orders from, Washington, D.C., through messages sent from this house. During World War II, when the Germans occupied France, the underground cable was destroyed by mutual agreement with the Allies so as not to fall into enemy hands. It was restored after the war."

Wow Factor

When asked about his wow factor, Ozon took me through the cluttered Operators' Room, filled with all sorts of telegraphs, teletypes, and other equipment, and showed me a small, worn brass keypad. It had two, large round discs on it, one for each finger to use. "I remember my dad, sitting here bent over this key press, tapping out important messages to high-ranking officials and businesses all around the country. On his shift there were only three people in the room. I would come down to watch him. He was very serious about getting the messages right. I can still see him in this chair," Ozon said, his voice trailing off. As we left, he turned and gently tapped out of a few letters on the same original piece of history that his father had used more than six decades before.

As for Manas's wow factor, he took a different approach. "Well, there are just so many elaborate, confusing pieces of electrical equipment here that I think I will choose this," he said as he pointed to a glass exhibit display.

In the case were all sorts of memorabilia that belonged to Cyrus

Field, the man credited with the success of the transatlantic cable. Advertisements, pieces of china, awards, and so on. At the top was a very curious item.

"That is my wow factor," Manas said with a grin. "It is an ornate Tiffany box engraved with Cyrus Field's name on it and the logo of his company. Inside the box is an actual piece of the transatlantic cable. He sold these as a fundraiser for his company. You can see, next to it, is a signed letter from him to the Tiffany Company verifying its authenticity. With all of his global impact, Mr. Field was also quite a showman. I think he made more money selling these souvenir Tiffany boxes with the cable in it than he did with his company."

The Takeaway

This little museum was one of the biggest surprises in my travels and research for this book. It is very heavy on the technical side, but having said that, it is impressive that many of the older, original pieces of equipment are still working and can be demonstrated. Something I particularly enjoyed seeing was the advancement of the transmitting machines. From the very early, clunky dot-and-dash teletypes to a later version that had ribbons with codes printed on them, the station here was at the forefront of then-modern techniques used in transmitting electric messages. One of the later ones, which can be demonstrated, allows the visitor to click out a key message, which then gets translated to a ribbon, which then gets sent to a machine where an actual ink pen, a new invention at the time, writes out the message in code.

The Nuts and Bolts

French Cable Station Museum

41 South Orleans Road (Route 28)
Orleans, Massachusetts 02653
(508) 240-1735
www.frenchcablestationmuseum.org
This museum is handicapped accessible.

Travel Suggestion

The museum backs up to the cove where the Orleans
Yacht Club is located.

Museum Hours

June through September: Friday through Sunday, 1 p.m.
to 4 p.m.; last tour at 3:30 p.m.
The museum is closed off-season. Special tours,
however, may be arranged.

Admission

Free

Up around the Bend

In the small village of Orleans you will enjoy visiting the Artist Cottages. These gaily colored faux sea-shanties are clustered together in an area known as Orleans Market Square. Artists, craftspeople, and others rent and decorate these little cottages by the season to sell their wares.

26 Mashpee Wampanoag Museum

Mashpee

"Let's begin our tour in the weety8," Carol Wynne told me. She is the cultural program developer for the Wampanoag Museum in Mashpee. "This weety8 [pronounced wee-two] was the center of family living for our tribe. It is a small roundhouse covered in bark in the winter and dry leaves in the warmer weather. Inside we see almost everything a Wampanoag family would have needed a couple of centuries ago. Everything was done outside, but the living quarters inside consisted of beds covered with animal furs, a fire pit for heating and cooking, a smoke hole for air and ventilation, and all of the family's other belongings would be hung on the curved walls." When I arrived for my tour the weety8 was still covered with intricately layered slabs of heavy bark. "When we bring schoolchildren out here for a visit, we

gather them all in a circle inside, and I begin to tell the story of our people and our culture. They are very focused as they sit in the dark surrounded by these artifacts," she said.

A long tableau along the hallway wall illustrates the timeline of Wampanoag leaders including many chiefs. These photographs are quite revealing. Many of the chiefs are in full Wampanoag regalia including face paint, feathers, headdresses, and jewelry. "These chiefs go back as far as we can find photographs for them. It is quite impressive when you see the years they governed and the positions they held in our tribe," Wynne said. "I enjoy looking at this timeline because I have several family members who are depicted on here." She pointed to sepia-toned photographs of two uncles who were chiefs and a cousin who was a medicine man. "They all had Anglicized names, but they also had native names, which you can see under the photos. They had regular lives outside of the tribe but were important leaders of the Wampanoags, too." She pointed to the names along the wall under the leaders' images: Drifting Goose, The World, Yellow Feather, Morning Star, Slow Turtle, and others. "Here is my relative Clinton Marcellus Haynes, who used the name Wild Horse. He actually went to school at the famed Carlisle [Pennsylvania] Indian Industrial School. He wanted to be a runner like the great Olympian Jim Thorpe, who also attended this school. Instead they taught him carpentry."

Wynne is of Wampanoag descent. She is a member of the Clan Mothers. "We are a circle of women who act as advisors to the tribe. We give input and guidance. The circle is usually made up of the elder women. We are each given a representative name: Beaver, Bear, Turtle, Eel, and Deer. I am the Otter."

The main museum is housed in a small, elegant home called the Bourne-Avant House. "This is one of the oldest houses in Mashpee. It was built in 1793, and for many years it was owned by Mabel

[Nakoomis] Avant, who was an important and beloved member of the Wampanoag nation. She held many positions, but most importantly she was a keeper of our tribe's history. She was revered by our people and she loved this old house. Old timers can still remember Mabel sitting in her easy chair over there writing poetry by the window," Wynne said, pointing to a window seat. The house retains the original hearth footprint from 1793, and many of the rooms are still configured as they were over the decades. This living room holds archival photos of Avant, an old pump organ from the Indian Meeting House, and Indian artwork and tapestries.

A second room features dramatic wall depictions of life among the Wampanoag through the years. "Our people were important whale hunters," Wynne noted as we stood in front of a very large, dynamic painting of a Wampanoag Indian whaling party catching a whale. It is an exciting image. "Whale hunting was very important to us. If you caught one large whale you were set for a very long time. And they used that whale for everything from food to oil to clothing."

Other exhibits show items dating back centuries from the tribe in Mashpee. The baskets are intricate, beautiful, and quite amazing. "We were master basket weavers. As you can see by these examples they are quite elegant. They were colored red using the dye from the blood sport plant. Also, some of these baskets were woven so tightly they could even carry water."

This is a wonderful little museum with interesting aspects to it both inside and out.

Wow Factor

After giving it much thought, Wynne said, "My wow factor is intangible. I have the honor of telling the story of my own people here in my own way. My parents and grandparents were from this tribe. This is the only place that Mashpee Wampanoag people can come and hear about Mashpee Wampanoag history from an actual Mashpee Wampanoag. It is my honor to do this. As I guide people around this museum, especially younger tribe members, it is so satisfying to hear them say, 'Oh, look. That is my Grandmother.' Or 'that was my teacher.' Or 'that is my cousin.' It makes it real to them. I tell them to go down the road to the Old Indian Meeting House. It is the oldest Indian church in America. I tell them to walk through the cemetery and experience the ancestry of our tribe. They get it. They understand. We have had a lot of new interest in our history from the younger ones since this museum was named to the National Register of Historic Places in 1998, and then when we became the newest federally recognized Indian tribe in 2007. We are teaching our ancestral language to them, and when you do that you bring back the culture, the music, the dance, the pride, and energy. I am so happy to be a part of all of this, and for that I choose this as my wow factor."

The Takeaway

Many people will first be introduced to this eastern Massachusetts/ Cape Cod tribe through a visit to this museum. There are many high-lights. The most impactful to me was the large diagram that tells the often sad story of the difficult life, a life akin to slavery, that this tribe suffered through over many years. For example, one of the largest exhibits relates how Wampanoag members toiled in the early days of whaling. The depiction of their story is quite harrowing. After the name of each whaler it states their fate: death from dysentery, died of yellow fever, froze to death, ship was burned by crew (disappeared), deserted, starved to death, shot by fellow crewmember, and mutiny.

It is a sobering exhibit to say the least. I would think this museum would attract a wide variety of visitors from road warriors to Cape Cod tourists to school groups. It is extremely well done and tells an important and little-known story in a compelling way.

The Nuts and Bolts

Mashpee Wampanoag Museum

414 Main Street   ·
Mashpee, Massachusetts 02649
(508) 477-9339
www.mashpeewampanoagtribe-nsn.gov/museum/
This museum is handicapped accessible.

Travel Suggestion

This museum is located along the Mashpee River just outside of the town's business district. A small community park is located two blocks from the museum. The park has walking paths, a gazebo, a one-room schoolhouse, and other interesting things to see.

Museum Hours

The museum is open seasonally, Monday through Friday, 10 a.m. to 4 p.m. The museum closes for the winter on December 1. Call in advance for any of the events the museum hosts. The largest of these is the annual July 4 Mashpee Wampanoag Powwow, which thousands attend.

Admission

Adults: $5.00
Children (6–18): $2.00
Family: $10.00
Seniors and educators: $4.00

Up around the Bend

A perfect companion visit to pair with this museum is the Old Indian Meeting House at 410 Meetinghouse Road, Mashpee. This is the oldest church on Cape Cod and the oldest Indian church in eastern North America. A walk through this churchyard cemetery reveals so much. This is the burying place for generations of the Wampanoag tribe, and a stroll through the cemetery to examine the gravestones will add to the narrative that you learned at the museum. Almost all of the stones carry both the English and Native American names of the deceased. Also noted are the leaders, chiefs, medicine men, clan mothers, and others who played significant roles in the tribe. The stones are adorned with Indian artwork, images, and the symbolic turtle. The combination of the museum and this venerable cemetery will give you new insight into one of Cape Cod's great and yet relatively unknown stories.

REGION FIVE
Central

Photograph by John Phelan. Creative Commons license available at:
https://creativecommons.org/licenses/by-sa/4.0/.

27 Fisher Museum at Harvard Forest

Petersham

⌒

This museum is like no other I have ever been to. The Fisher Museum is surrounded by the Harvard Forest. And this is no ordinary woods.

"Harvard University purchased thousands of acres of woods here in Petersham in 1907," said Greta Van Scoy, museum assistant. "Since that time, this forest, now around 3,700 acres, has become one of the oldest monitored forests in North America. Researchers, international scholars, foresters, students, and others have been monitoring basically every inch of this forest for over a century. We have research sites throughout, plus several tall towers in the forest which record and sometimes video the happenings in there. Much information can be gleaned from this data such as land use techniques, ecological rejuvenation, the impact of wildlife on the forest, and other subject matter, all of which have been studied here. We have several eight-foot tall exclosures, which keep deer and moose out of a restricted area so we can monitor the forest without the impact of the animals, to see how forests manage to take care of themselves. It really is fascinating."

Okay, but moose?

"We have had several moose sightings on our cameras and also in person. In fact, I once came upon a whole family of them. A bull moose, a cow, and her two calves. They walked right up to me."

Van Scoy escorted me on a short walk up to the forest entrances. It was gorgeous, to say the least. A fenced-in area held everything from longhorn cattle to tall weather stations. A group of several women in vests and red hardhats were learning the art of tree climbing on one end of the field. The forest ahead of us was rich and lush and thick with old red oaks and red maple trees.

"Our forest is very much alive. We still tap the old sugar maples. Our cameras tell us that the woods are full of animals, and we have seen images of turkeys, bobcats, bear, and more."

It was clear to me that Van Scoy felt a deep kinship to Harvard Forest and to her job.

"Richard Fisher was a Harvard Professor of Forestry, and he was the driving force behind the university acquiring the forest for research purposes. I love being in the outdoors, experiencing nature up close and doing field research. And to do that as a job is just fantastic."

As wondrous and interesting as Harvard Forest is in all its splendor, another marvel of sorts can be found inside the staid red brick walls of the Fisher Museum.

"It really is all about the dioramas," Van Scoy said.

We soon found ourselves in a large room inside the building.

The walls are lined with the most amazing miniature dioramas imaginable. There are twenty-three of them. They document the history of a typical forest, over several centuries, in the southern New England area. The exactitude of each diorama must be seen to be believed.

"These were created between 1931 and 1941 by Guernsey and Pitman's studio in Cambridge, Massachusetts. They were the premier diorama makers of their era. The first seven dioramas basically show a walk in the woods, the same woods, over different periods of time. The forest can be seen to begin, progress, regress, reform, and change in so many ways."

The first dioramas appear to depict the same exact landscape covering a span of 230 years. They are large, easily viewable, and well lit. There are hundreds of trees in each one, and you can vividly see the changing of the habitat over the years. Every tiny tree can be identified by species. In the first diorama you can see the area around Petersham basically raw, covered with trees and populated by a few Native Americans. In the next one (depicting a forty-year jump) you can see trees being cleared for farming. Then a farmhouse and other buildings appear. Trees get cut down for building lumber and new forests sprout up. Roads appear. Fields are being tended. Later in time, we see the fields being abandoned as the focus shifted away from family farms. Soon neglect takes over the land. Then, again, a rebirth with a display of new techniques and life begins again as a valuable pine forest grows and begins to be harvested on this same patch of land. The illustration of the passage of time is quite dramatic.

What make this whole viewing experience so fascinating is that the creators populated each diorama with vignettes from rural New England life. We can observe miniature workers planting crops and miniature horses pulling wagons. A man and his dog are shown hunting in the woods. We see a whole array of tiny vintage cars and pickup trucks going down the country roads. The fields are dotted with little foxes, horses, and cows. At the mill, workers are busy sawing timber.

"Look, down here," Van Scoy said. She was pointing to the corner of one of the later dioramas. It was a man sitting in a chair in the woods. "That is Professor Fisher himself, just sitting on a rock marveling at his forest in front of him."

As we slowly moved along the walls I felt a curious kinship with those in each diorama. I felt as if I came to know the early farmers, the teenagers who would move off the family homestead, the workers creating a prosperous living in the New England frontier. I felt joy when the forest was robust and full of leafy grandeur. I felt a tinge of sadness at seeing the diorama that shows the once-sturdy farmhouse now forgotten and dilapidated. There is much to understand about the resilience of nature from these dioramas. There is no question that, when the forest is left to itself, it tends to take care of itself, adapt, and survive.

By the time I got to the last diorama, which depicts a forest fire ripping through the landscape, I felt an emotional connection to this cherished, "imaginary" piece of land. Miniature fireman can be seen dragging hoses through the brush from their firetrucks trying to beat back the flames. An old wooden fire tower looms forlornly above everything.

"Yes, that fire tower still stands even today," Van Scoy observed quietly.

A final, separate diorama shows how the artisans created them. In minute detail visitors can see how the trees, the landscape, and all that is in each window were made. The main components in the making of these treasures are clay, paint, and miles of copper wires, used to make the trees.

Wow Factor

"I really enjoy the faces on the kids when they visit here. They are so interested in everything. They can't stop saying wow all the time. We do a lot of tours here. School groups, especially the smaller ones, just fall in love with the dioramas. In fact we send them on a Diorama Scavenger Hunt. It is fun to watch them. The scavenger hunt allows the children to peer more intently into each diorama. To really study each one. The sheet they are given asks them to find and identify eighteen different items. Among them are cattails, a woodpecker, a man lighting his pipe (Professor Fisher), a rabbit, a lunch box, a dog with a bird, and an outhouse! It is a lot of fun for all of us," Van Scoy said.

I also asked Clarisse Hart what her wow factor is. She is the outreach and education director of the Harvard Forest. "The dioramas are really incredible to look at. But for me, the real amazing artifact that we have is an actual 1930s-era 16mm film of them being made. It is fascinating. You can see these artisans hard at work, creating the topography, painting the backdrops, molding the figures. They are so exact and deft in their work. You can see them form each little tree out of a piece of wire, starting with the branches and then down the trunk. It was painstaking work, but they were masters of their craft and it is obvious when you see the film." The film is available for viewing on a monitor near the dioramas, and it clearly demonstrates that they had a deep love and understanding of the physiology of each tree.

I asked Hart if she agreed with Van Scoy that it was also a wow factor to watch the kids undertake their scavenger hunts.

"Yes, but it is so frustrating," she chuckled. "It took me three years to find that darned woodpecker in a diorama. And the kids always find it right away!"

The Takeaway

The woods out behind the museum are open to the public and easily accessible to all. Inside the main buildings are a number of rooms, most of them private. Researchers from all over the world come here to study and do exacting research, so there are living quarters for them to stay for a length of time. In that regard, it is similar to a college campus and dormitory. The large communal rooms are comfortable, and there are many areas and warrens where students and researchers can hole up with their books and data. The Fisher Museum, which is the diorama section, takes up a separate wing of the main building.

This is an interesting place that I liked a lot. On a nice day, a walk through Harvard Forest is incredibly enjoyable. The dioramas inside are unique among the items I encountered in the writing of this book.

The Nuts and Bolts

Fisher Museum at Harvard Forest

324 North Main Street
Petersham, Massachusetts 01366
(978) 724-3302
http://harvardforest.fas.harvard.edu/fisher-museum
This museum is handicapped accessible.

Travel Suggestion

Petersham is just a small community of about 1,200 residents. The best way to get here is off of Route 2, which runs east to west about five miles north of the hamlet. Route 32 is Main Street. Signage is scant for Fisher Museum, so keep your eye out for it on your left coming from Route 2.

Museum Hours

November through April: Monday to Friday, 9 a.m. to 4 p.m.
May through October: Monday to Friday, 9 a.m. to 4 p.m.; Saturday and Sunday, 12 p.m. to 4 p.m.

Admission

Free

Up around the Bend

The Stone Cow Brewery is located about eight miles southeast of Petersham in Barre. Situated on a thousand-acre family farm, the brewery is known for its craft beers, food products, and activities, which include farm tours, food events, and live music.

28 Willard House and Clock Museum

North Grafton

This museum is located in the former homestead of the Willard brothers, Benjamin, Simon, Ephraim, and Aaron. Each of them gets the spotlight here in a veritable "World of Clocks."

"They were an amazing family," said Patrick Keenan, director. "Each of them had twelve children. They were real artisans, with Simon being the most famous of them all. They were among the premier clockmakers of their era, and to own a Willard was to own a treasure. One has to remember that the Willards made clocks in a period when not everybody had a timepiece in their home. Clocks were very expensive and usually were featured prominently in a person's home. And we have many wonderful examples of them all right here at the museum."

The Willards were innovators and far ahead of their time, at least in the field of clock-making. They were early colonial makers of the eight-day clock as well as the banjo-shaped clocks that are popular with collectors (they are formally known as Improved Timepiece Clocks). This is usually a tall clock with a round clock face on top and a narrowing column with a square glass base on it. The base is many times painted or embossed. This was the first commercially successful wall clock in America.

"It was a remarkable invention. In fact, we have Willard's patent here for everybody to see," Keenan said as he pointed to a framed piece of parchment on the wall. "This is a copy of the original patent for the clock." The document describes the clock's workings and is dated 1802. "We like this because the patent was issued during an era when patents were not numbered but rather were signed to certify them. The patent is signed by both John Adams and James Madison. The Willards were friends with many of those in high positions of that era. In this room we can also see an engraved walking stick that was owned by President James Madison and presented to the brothers."

The clock galleries are really magnificent showrooms. Clocks of all sizes are quietly ticking away on floors, on walls, on shelves, and in cases. The clock pieces are decorative, the artwork is creative, and the clocks themselves are stunning pieces of furniture. At the front door visitors are greeted with a harbinger of what is to come. It is a massive tall clock (we know them today as grandfather clocks). It was constructed of gleaming mahogany in 1770. The clock face reads, "Benj. Willard, Grafton." It towers over the original low-ceilinged room at eight-feet tall and has brass finials along the top, an eight-day timepiece, a calendar window, and a separate second-hand clock. The others on display in the following rooms are just as magnificent.

"One of my favorites is the Aaron Willard Rocking Ship Clock,"

Keenan said as we entered another gallery room. This beauty stood nine feet tall and featured images of ships rocking across the waves in time with the pendulum beats. Other clocks in this room include a massive gallery clock taken from the Old Boylston Market Building in Boston. It features a gold-leaf edged, five-by-five-foot circular clock adorned with a gilded eagle finial. Another large wall clock was taken from the 1804 First Church of Roxbury, Massachusetts. Atop the clock face is a large eagle. In each of its talons it holds thirteen gold-colored spheres signifying the original colonies.

I remarked at the beauty of each of these masterpieces.

"They are quite valuable and rare. In Washington, D.C., there is a Willard clock in the White House, two in Congress, and one very large one in the U.S. Supreme Court."

I asked the director if the ticking of so many timepieces all at once makes him a little edgy at times.

"Oh, no. I really love this place. If I am gone from the museum for a couple of days and come back and have to wind all of the clocks at once, well, it's that silence that is really unnerving to me," he said. "To me these clocks are living things. To think that some of them have been keeping time for over 250 years is incredible. I mean, what today is going to be still working, something made by human hands, in another 250 years? We don't have the great craftsmen like they had in that era. If you stop and think about it, I am winding clocks that have been wound by people dating back to the Declaration of Independence!"

Wow Factor

"The musical clocks are of particular interest to me," Keenan told me. "Remember, the only time there was music in one's home in those days was if you paid for someone to come into your home and play for you, knew someone who would play for you, or you would have to play music for yourself. So to bring music into a home via a clock is really special. They were the Rolls-Royce of the clock industry. Some public places, like taverns, would buy a musical clock and then charge customers to play it. So really, you could say that a musical clock was the first jukebox."

There is one particular musical clock at the museum that is quite intriguing. It is also the largest clock in the collection. It was made by brother Simon, and it plays seven different songs.

"They were the hits of the time, I guess. Some of the titles were 'Lady Coventry's Minuet,' 'Bold Highland Laddy,' 'Nancy Dawson,' 'Buttered Peas,' the '149th Psalm,' and some popular marching songs. Some were pretty risqué for the time. In fact, Nancy Dawson was a big entertainer of that era who shocked the public by showing her ankles while she danced to these," he said.

The Takeaway

This is a very interesting museum housed in a companion historic building. The Willard homestead was a lively place with all of the family members around and the brothers always making their clocks. There are period-appointed rooms to view, including bedrooms, a kitchen, and a keeping room. Antiques, including several original Willard items, are numerous. The clock galleries are beautiful display areas, and the majestic clocks are completely fascinating to watch. Keenan and his associates are well versed in the Willard clock story, and they give a fascinating tour.

Don't miss the Willards' clock shop where the entire clock-making was done. Things have changed little around this part of Grafton according to Keenan. He told me that the view from the clock shop window hasn't changed at all since the brothers were in there tinkering away two centuries ago.

A well-stocked gift shop sells many clock-themed items as well as books, children's items, and, of course, clocks.

The Nuts and Bolts

Willard House and Clock Museum

11 Willard Street
North Grafton, Massachusetts 01536
(508) 839-3500
www.willardhouse.org
This museum is handicapped accessible.

Travel Suggestion

As you are searching for the Willard Clock Museum (there are signs), you will be passing the Cummings School of Veterinary Medicine. This school sprawls over several hundred acres bordering Willard Street. It is a part of Tufts University and is the only veterinary college in New England.

Museum Hours

April 1 through December 31: Wednesday to Saturday, 10 a.m. to 4 p.m.; Sunday, 1 p.m. to 4 p.m.
January 1 through March 31: Friday and Saturday, 10 a.m. to 4 p.m.; Sunday, 1 p.m. to 4 p.m.

Admission

Adults: $10.00
Seniors (60+): $9.00
Children (6–12): $6.00

Up around the Bend

Grafton (three miles south of the museum) is a lovely little New England town. On a warm sunny day it can be a relaxing place for strolling the village square (known as a common), learning about some of the many historic buildings in the quaint downtown area, or even having lunch at the historic, three-story Grafton Inn (1801). Also, the J. Cheney Wells Clock Gallery is located at Old Sturbridge Village just twenty-five miles southwest of North Grafton. This museum houses dozens of classic old timepieces including many early grandfather clocks.

29 Clara Barton Birthplace Museum

⟶

North Oxford

Emily Thomas has her dream job.

"I admire Clara Barton," she told me. Thomas is the docent researcher for this museum. "We have some parallels to our lives. Like her, I am from Oxford. I have a great interest in women's issues. I teach Women's Medicine, Women in American Society, and Human Rights at nearby Nichols College. Clara was also a teacher in her early days. Clara was the youngest of five children, and so am I!"

I asked Professor Thomas if Clara's story is well-known in the area.

"Most certainly. She is, after all, the most famous woman to come out of Oxford. All of the locals know her and are proud of her. Even at my college, all the young people know Clara's

Photograph by Daderot. Creative Commons license available at:
https://creativecommons.org/publicdomain/zero/1.0/.

biography. We feel a strong connection to her. We walk the same streets that she did. She was a worldwide celebrity, and yet she called this little corner of Massachusetts home. I am her number one fan," she said.

Thomas led me on a timeline tour of the Barton homestead. She is a treasure trove of details, small stories, historical minutiae, and fun factoids concerning "America's Angel of Mercy."

The first room is the summer kitchen, filled with period furniture. The Bartons raised carriage horses and were considered to be modestly well off. Although Clara herself never had children, the house was obviously the center of many lively Barton family gatherings over the years.

In the next room, the dining room, we find several items that belonged to Barton personally. Her infant high chair is here, as is a school bell she treasured. But there was one possession that Clara held in most high regard.

"In this cabinet we have a beautiful red paper fan. Clara bought it during a trip to France. She just loved this fan and was very protective of it. When her nieces and nephews came for a visit, she would let them play with many of the items and toys in the house. But everybody knew that her red fan was off-limits!"

Also on display in this cabinet is a handwritten receipt for the first semester of college for Clara's niece Sally. It was for Nichols College (then Academy), totaling $20.21. For the entire semester.

The next room is a more formal parlor. Here we find several stunning items. One of them is Clara Barton's actual Civil War field desk.

"Clara would lug this thing all over the battlefield. She would set it up, open the doors, and record her findings and daily experiences in her medical journal. When she was done she would pack it up and move to another area where the battle was ongoing. I guess you could call it 'her laptop computer,'" Thomas smiled. "We know that Clara was in the thick of it during these battles, tending to the wounded and aiding the soldiers. A famous story tells of the time she was tending to a casualty at the battle of Antietam when a Confederate bullet pierced the sleeve of her blouse and unfortunately struck and killed the soldier she was nursing. She was a true heroine during the war."

On the wall in the parlor is an object that will give any history buff a pause. It is a large, framed legal commission raising Clara's brother, David, to the rank of captain. It is dated 1862 and hand-signed by President Abraham Lincoln.

It is breathtaking.

Wow Factor

In this home filled with wow factors, many of them large, personal items of Barton's, my guide took me into the last room of the tour and showed me perhaps one of the smallest items in the house.

A little green pail.

"It looks like a little toy, but it is not," Thomas told me. "This little green pail, maybe only five inches wide, belonged to Clara. She was a big pet lover, and in particular she liked cats. One of her favorite cats was named Tommy. Although Clara was a tireless world-traveler she always regretted leaving Tommy at home. She would put a couple of dollars in this little green pail for the caretakers to use to buy Tommy cat treats while she was gone. I just love this little pail; it is just so personal and so charming. It really humanizes this legendary woman. It brings her down to a level we can all understand. Sure, she was one of the most famous women in the world, but she was also a sentimental lady who really missed her kitty when she was gone. It is a sweet item unlike almost anything else we have at the museum."

The Takeaway

I found that I walked around this museum with my mouth open in astonishment. There are so many historical items here that you almost become numb to them. The battlefield desk. The precious red fan. An original Red Cross uniform. Clara's personal passport for her trip to Russia. The Lincoln-signed commission. Any fan of history will want to take this tour nice and slow to drink in the sheer importance of the house's contents.

For me, there was one item that rose above them all. Thomas finished our tour in what she called the "birthing room." Clara was born in this room, and her original bed is still here. But it is what is on that bed that really captured my attention.

"The quilt on this bed is priceless," the researcher told me. "It was hand-stitched and is quite colorful and elaborate. But look at the names on it. Each panel is inscribed with the name of one of her colleagues, veterans, and officers that Clara served with in the Civil War. These veterans presented the quilt to her in the 1870s. We had it inspected by a group of fabric experts in New Jersey in 2003. They concluded that this was in fact original from that era."

The squares of the quilt read like a Who's Who of the Civil War. One patch is from General John Logan (the founder of Memorial Day), others are from General A. E. Burnside (who was a general, a Rhode Island senator and governor, and the first president of the National Rifle Association), General A. B. Underwood (commander of the 33rd Massachusetts regiment at Gettysburg), General Zenas

Bliss (a Medal of Honor recipient), and General Charles Devens (a large Massachusetts army base is named in his honor).

There are many wonderful, famous homes and birthplace museums in Massachusetts. This one is excellent.

The Nuts and Bolts

Clara Barton Birthplace Museum

66 Clara Barton Road
North Oxford, Massachusetts 01537
(508) 987-2056, ext. 2013
www.clarabartonbirthplace.org
This museum is handicapped accessible.

Travel Suggestion

The museum is located seven miles southwest of the city of Worcester. Her home is adjacent to a large camp for young people who have diabetes. Clara Barton, who did not have the disease, funded this camp, and it carries a full camping and activity schedule all summer.

Museum Hours

May 26 through August 27: Friday to Sunday, 10 a.m. to 4 p.m.
September: Saturday, 10 a.m. to 4 p.m.
Other dates and times by appointment only.

Admission

Adults: $6.00
Children (6–12): $3.00
AAA members and seniors: $5.00

Up around the Bend

No visit to this museum would be complete without a trip to Clara Barton's final resting place, just a mile from the museum. The small North Cemetery is located at 505 Main Street, Oxford. The Barton family plot is large and easy to find. Across the top it reads, "Clara Barton: Angel of the Battlefield." Next to it is a large monument with a bright red cross on top.

Photograph by Peter Vanderwarker.

30 Museum of Russian Icons

Clinton

The phrase "one of a kind" is thrown about pretty casually in the world of museums and historical artifacts. However, the exemplification of that timeworn phrase can be found right here in Clinton, Massachusetts.

The Museum of Russian Icons is unlike anything you will find in the United States, if not the world.

"An icon is a sacred object used for prayer," museum director Kent Russell told me. "They stem from the earliest ages of Christianity. Even the most basic symbols of faith, like the fish, for example, date from the dawning of the Christian culture. These icons have remained unchanged as an art form for centuries. They are all handmade, so no two are alike. We have over one thousand icons, with more than three hundred always on display."

These venerable artifacts can be hypnotizing to view. Always painted on carefully chosen wood, the faces, particularly the eyes, seek you out as if to invite you back to an ancient era. The colors are surprisingly bright and always painted in egg tempera.

"Again, the symbolism. The egg because it represents the beginning of life. In fact, there isn't a piece of an icon, no matter how big or small, that doesn't have symbolism. They are more than art. To study an icon is to study a language. They are much closer to scripture than to a painting."

Each icon features a religious figure like Jesus Christ, Mary, or any of the saints of the church. A typical icon has a single figure on it, but others can have hundreds of figures.

"Some of these are what we call liturgical calendars," Russell said as he walked me over to an extravagant example. "This is known as the Minyeia Liturgical Calendar. As you can see, there are dozens and dozens of small figures painted across the front of the icon. There are 365 saints here, a different saint for each day of the year. Around the border we find three hundred different interpretations of the Mothers of God. The detailing of each tiny figure is precise right down to the facial features. It is a remarkable work of art."

The size of the icons in the museum range from smaller ones you might find in a person's home to the largest one, titled Christ in Majesty, which is five feet by four feet in size. This would have been a centerpiece in a Russian church. All are spectacular. Highlights include *Three Marys at the Sepulcher* (1480), *John the Baptist* (1450), and one of the most complex known icons, *The Last Judgment* (1650).

"*The Last Judgment* is one of our most important works of art. As you can see, it's filled with iconography. It is a massive thematic depiction of the Old and New Testaments and the Gospel stories. It has too many figures in it to even count. We can see Christ, Mary, saints, Adam and Eve, Satan, John the Baptist, and dozens more. The detail is exquisite. Notice that in the lap of Satan we can even see Judas holding a bag of coins, his payment for the betrayal of Christ. Truly a remarkable piece."

The museum building provides a modern setting for these ancient works of sacred art. The displays are reverentially lit, and each icon is showcased for the maximum effect. There is a large display room that holds revolving Russian-themed exhibits. On the day of my visit, this room held a display of silver samovars as well as dozens of exquisitely carved Russian nesting dolls, for example.

As Russell guided me from room to room, we came upon a scholarly looking older gentleman who was standing alone admiring a particular icon. Russell introduced me to him, and we shook hands. Russell explained to him that I was writing a book which will feature the museum, and the gentleman whispered to me, "We are most grateful," and quietly walked away.

"Who was that man?" I asked.

"He is the reason this museum exists. His name is Gordon Lankton, and he is the founder of the museum. He is the owner of Nypro, a billion-dollar plastics company which is located across the street from the museum. He is eighty-five years old now, and comes to his museum almost every day. His company does business in 17 countries around the world including Russia. Early on, he took an interest in Russian icons and started purchasing them and bringing them back to his home here. Eventually he desired a permanent place to house and exhibit his collection, so he bought this old building and started renovating it. This building dates from the 1840s and was once a part of the Bigelow Carpet manufacturing factory, the largest of its kind in the world. Later, it would be an administration building, a post office, a courthouse, and now this beautiful museum. Mr. Lankton was involved in every step of the transformation into what you see today, the largest and finest collection of Russian icons outside of Moscow."

Wow Factor

"For sheer magnificence, the Smolensk *Mother of God* is without peer," Russell began. "It was created in 1690. The icon itself is fantastic in its depiction of Mary. It is extra rare in that it is signed by the artist. It is almost unheard of to find something this old which identifies the painter. It says on it, 'Painted by the Monk FILARET.' Adding even more to this gorgeous icon is that we have its cover. The cover was an elaborately carved and designed top to protect the icon. This one is completely created in gold plating and silver, and it is covered in precious jewels." The director pointed out diamonds, topaz, sapphires, aquamarines, rubies, and more to me.

The Takeaway

A lasting impression I got from this museum, besides all the wondrous artifacts it holds, is the museum itself. It is an amazing example of architectural repurposing of an old building. The interior is elegant and not wanting of any accessory. In fact, there is a library off the main floor that holds an extensive collection of books dedicated to icons. The shelves go from floor to ceiling. To reach the top shelf you climb a custom-made moveable ladder from Switzerland.

All of this is a tribute to Lankton's dedication to historical preservation. In the basement there are research rooms used as private study centers. These are actually located inside several old jail cells from the time when the building was used as a courthouse. The iron bars of the cell doors are still in place.

I was also very impressed by the small army of volunteer docents on staff during my visit. At least a half dozen of these were all giving guided tours around the museum to the individuals and groups in attendance this busy day. Each docent was extremely well-versed in the subject matter, and they made the tours come alive for the youth groups, art groups, and senior groups visiting the museum.

A well-stocked gift shop carries tasteful souvenirs of the museum, from jewelry to posters to the ever-popular Russian nesting dolls.

The Nuts and Bolts

Museum of Russian Icons
203 Union Street
Clinton, Massachusetts 01510
(978) 598-5000
www.museumofrussianicons.org
This museum is handicapped accessible.

Travel Suggestion
Free and metered parking can be found on the streets near the museum.

Museum Hours
Tuesday through Friday, 11 a.m. to 4 p.m.;
weekends, 11 a.m. to 5 p.m.

Admission
Adults: $10.00
Seniors (59+): $7.00
Students and children (3–17): $5.00

Up around the Bend

A perfect way to unwind and reflect on your visit to this museum is to stroll Clinton's Central Park, which is directly across the street. This four-acre park has shade trees, landscaping, and benches, and it features a historic sundial and two war monuments paying tribute to locals who died in the Spanish-American War and the Civil War. A large, ornate fountain in the center has a great history. It was given to Clinton by John R. Foster in 1890. It was destroyed in a hurricane in 1938 and a replica replaced it.

31 Massachusetts State Police Museum and Learning Center

South Grafton

"Few people realize that the Massachusetts State Police is the oldest statewide police agency in the country. We began on May 16, 1865. So with that much history behind our badges and uniforms it is fitting that we have this museum here to tell our story," Charlie Alejandro said. Alejandro, known to her friends as "Shirl," is the museum director. She is also a retired twenty-year veteran of the Massachusetts State Police (MSP).

The museum, though small and still in its growing phase, has numerous exhibits, displays, and memorabilia from virtually every era of the department—even dating back to the "horse era."

"Yes, obviously, horses played an important part in the early

years of the department. Long before vehicles came around horses were vital in police protection, and the MSP used them extensively. We have several original saddles on display here from that time. It is funny now, but imagine this. Back in the day each horse was issued an official warrant making it an actual police officer. Horses were used for nearly a century in our state. Our last police horse 'officer,' Teddy, died in 1947."

John "Jack" Crawford is a member of the museum's board of directors. "This museum is important to our state's history," he told me. "We have many events each year, and we are always looking to add to our collections. Many retired members of the force come by here to reminisce. The stories they tell, from twenty, thirty, and even forty years ago, are incredible. When this old building, a former troop barracks, became available we sought it with the idea of housing our museum. You might not know it now, but the road out front was once one of the busiest in the state. It was the main road to Cape Cod, so it saw a lot of action."

Crawford, like Alejandro, knows of what he speaks. "I am privileged to be the only officer who worked in our original barracks building at every rank—trooper, corporal, sergeant, staff sergeant, station commander, and lieutenant."

The museum has several exhibit areas on the main floor. Display cases hold hundreds of archival photographs, memorabilia, uniforms, commendations, and vintage police equipment. It is a nice touch that tours are given by volunteers as well as retired officers, many of whom actually worked in the original Troop C building less than a mile away.

The museum holds several public events each year to raise funds and awareness of their mission. The most popular event by far is the old police vehicle show they hold on the grounds.

"Those events are spectacular," Alejandro told me. "People from many states drive their classic police vehicles here to display them. It is quite a scene. Cars from the 1940s and 1950s, with the one big light on the roof and those old classic police decals on the door. Just great. People swarmed the place. The kids in town loved it. Cars from every agency, from many states show up. We have old police motorcycles, utility vehicles, and even some old police snowmobiles are on display. I think the farthest they have come from is Virginia. We had almost forty vehicles at our biggest show. It was a wonderful day."

Wow Factor

Both Crawford and Alejandro weighed in on their personal wow factors at the museum.

"Look at this dinosaur," Crawford said as he walked me over to a large metal-gray teletype machine. "This is the real deal. Keypad and all. I actually worked this machine back in the 1960s when I was a young trooper. It really shows how police technology has progressed. I would get a report of a crime or a missing person or something. Then I would come over here and type out the report or bulletin and send it out to agencies around the area. You had to be very careful. The message was printed out laboriously on a long ribbon, and if you made a little mistake you had to start all over again. No delete button back then. We had to use this machine because it was the most secure way of getting important messages out. We couldn't use phones because they could be unreliable. Heck, back then we even had party lines so anybody could listen in. In fact, when we were using our line nobody else could make a call. Yes, this was a vital and important part of our mission in those days. And it is very rare to have one." The museum has three of them.

For Alejandro, the wow factor is more sentimental. She took me into a large display room.

"We used to call this the Four Corners Room," she said. "In this room we have a mannequin dressed in the actual uniform of one of the four individual agencies that represented the Massachusetts State Police before they were all merged in 1992. In one corner the Capitol Police, then Registry Police, State Police, and finally the Metropolitan Police. Each one represents a proud history of police work in the state. We have visitors who seek out the uniform of the unit they worked in. They are amazed to see these rare uniforms all in one place. The Capitol Police officers remember the time they guarded Prince Charles or Nelson Mandela, for example. The Registry Police remember the early days of motor vehicle registration and early vehicle laws. We love to hear the stories. Our board of directors insists that we preserve the history of all departments."

The Takeaway

It was fun to hear my two interview subjects come up with their wow factors. But the truth is that there are many different ones to choose from here. For me, it would have to be an ungainly contraption located near the center of the main floor. It is one of the earliest pieces of police photographic equipment.

"Can you imagine," Crawford said. "This monstrosity was used to take mug shots over a half a century ago." I remarked that it looked like a torture instrument. "Well, the suspect had to sit in this unwieldy chair and hold still for as long as ten minutes. It has a head rest where they would put their head in position so as not to move. The two big lights in front would explode in a blast of light to try and capture his image. It is really something, isn't it? And, we are told, it still works. But, we haven't tried it out yet."

Perhaps my favorite area of the museum is actually the first exhibit you see on entering. When I saw it I was immediately struck with a sense of déjà-vu. In a stunning artist's recreation stands a vintage Howard Johnson diner counter. In front are two 1950s green leather stools. And then it dawned on me. I've seen this before. In a Norman Rockwell painting!

"Rockwell painted 'The Runaway' for a *Saturday Evening Post* cover in 1958," Alejandro said. "It showed a Massachusetts State Police officer sitting on a small stool next to a young boy who said he was running away from home. According to the Norman Rockwell Museum it is one of the artist's most popular paintings. Since a Massachusetts trooper is featured in the painting we decided to recreate the scene here at the museum. The setting is exact. Fathers and their children come and sit on the stools next to each other and have their photograph taken. It is a very popular part of our museum."

I asked her if she has any special memory from this exhibit.

"I sure do. One time both of the subjects of the painting came here together to see it. Retired trooper Dick Clemens and the little boy, Eddie Locke, came here and greeted our staff and visitors. It was a very emotional day for everybody." (Officer Clemens died in 2012 at the age of eighty-three).

The Nuts and Bolts

**Massachusetts State Police Museum
and Learning Center**

308 Providence Road
South Grafton, Massachusetts 01560
Website: www.mspmlc.org
Phone: (888) 707-4011
This museum is handicapped accessible.

Note: This museum suffered a fire on February 25, 2017. This caused them to move from their longstanding location to a new address. If you have visited this museum before, you might want to go back again. There are new displays and a whole new arrangement of the museum (as described in this chapter).

Travel Suggestion

This museum is located about five miles south of the Massachusetts Turnpike at Exit 11 on Route 122.

Museum Hours

Tuesday and Thursday, 11 a.m. to 2 p.m.;
Sunday, 12 p.m. to 3 p.m.

Admission

Call for single and group rates.

Up around the Bend

Sutton, Massachusetts, situated five miles west of the museum, is the home of the state's oldest candy maker, Eaton Farm Confectioners (1892).

32 Top Fun Aviation Toy Museum

~~~~~~~~~~

Fitchburg

A thread that runs true in more than a couple of the museums in this book is that they have sprung from a single person's hobby or collection and grown into a small museum of its own.

There is no better example of that than this little museum located on a side street in downtown Fitchburg, Massachusetts.

"It all started with simple enough intentions," Deborah L. Scheetz told me. She is the program director and a board member of the Top Fun Aviation Toy Museum. "Back in the 1980s, I got my private pilot's license. It was something I always wanted to do. Well, to celebrate this happy occasion all of my friends gifted me with toy planes of all different sizes. I kept them and continued to add to my collection over the years. After a while I started to keep a keen eye out for aviation toys and began collecting in earnest.

I went to flea markets, auctions, antique stores, and more. And from that grew all of this," she said as she swept her hand over the showroom floor of the small museum.

. We have all acquired a lot of "stuff" over the years and perhaps been faced with the question of where to put it. Scheetz solved that by taking over a large storefront and filling it with display cases and exhibit tables.

"Somehow, we keep adding to our collection at the museum. We have over 2,500 aviation toys and we are still counting. We really do not have a collection fund or budget. In fact, we don't have much of a budget at all," she laughed. "But we carry on. A half-dozen times a year someone will walk in with a box of old toy planes to donate. Things from their childhood or toys left to them from a deceased relative. Of course, we gladly accept them."

Scheetz's partner in all this is Rosalie Dunbar, the museum curator. A tiny, stooped, white-haired lady, Dunbar is about as close to an aviation toy expert as you can get. She was my tour guide for the afternoon.

"We have a myriad of types and styles of aviation toys," she began. "We have large ride-upon toys, we have new pop icon aviation toys like Barbie and Star Wars planes, and we have old tin toys from the Depression era. Some of our toys are little simple balsa wood aircraft made for about a dime. Others are much more elaborate."

"Bring out the Polly Pocket," Dunbar hollered to Scheetz.

We walked over to a large case, and the director brought a sleek, bright-colored plastic carrying case out to demonstrate. After she donned white gloves ("natural oils and grease, don't you know," she said authoritatively), she began to unravel the toy. Lifting the top off, she slid the wings out, pulled on several levers, flipped a few plastic tabs, and the whole thing evolved into an elaborate

Polly Pocket fashion show plane. There was a model runway with lights and mirrors, several small dressing rooms, a grand staircase, and an elevator to transport the models from the fashion runway down to the changing rooms. Overseeing all of this was Polly Pocket herself, sitting in a helicopter (for a fast getaway?) on a platform above the fashion show.

"This cost about ninety dollars brand new around the year 2001. We have actually had engineers come in to view it, and their jaws drop. The miniature detail is really quite remarkable," Dunbar told me.

She is also responsible for making the dioramas that illustrate several of the toy planes in action. Sea rescue planes hover over the choppy waters waiting to pluck a desperate seaman out of a storm-tossed ocean, for example. Other dioramas include scenes depicting aviation toys during the space race, battlefield actions, and more.

While most of the toys are clearly from somebody's toy box, others have real historical significance. There is a large selection of toys that were marketed to celebrate Charles Lindbergh's historic 1927 flight across the Atlantic Ocean, as well as others that pay tribute to the Wright brothers and Amelia Earhart.

"It is probably not much in the grand scheme of museums," Dunbar told me. "Still, we are proud of what we have accomplished here. All ages happen in, and we like to share stories with them of the toys of their past. We try and keep ourselves relevant by inviting in speakers and school groups. We have an activity room for the younger ones, and where we also have workshops and presentations. And we just keep on keeping on. And we've done pretty well for ourselves. In fact, we believe we are the only toy aviation museum in the world. And right here in Fitchburg."

Wow Factor

"That is hard. I have so many favorites in here," Scheetz said. "But I do like this one in particular."

She walked me over to a case that was crowded with hundreds of toy planes. She pointed to a toy on the bottom shelf. It was perhaps the smallest plane in the museum.

"I just love that little plane. It is nothing special. It is a tin toy plane from the 1930s, and it may be the oldest toy in the whole place. I just like it because as you can see, it has been well-used. Imagine a small child playing with that tiny toy in their bedroom back in the days of the Great Depression. Oh, the joy. You can see how used, how handled it is. To me it exemplifies the magic of toys, the universal appeal of childhood playthings. Clearly a child desired to have this toy, to play with this toy. To love it. We know that over the years toys get dropped, lost, broken, or even thrown away. But this little guy is still here right here in our museum. He is a survivor. Nothing spectacular, for sure. But that tiny tin plane is emblematic of what we try to do. To be the keepers of the memories of our youth."

"I just love that little plane," she repeated.

The Takeaway

The Top Fun Aviation Toy Museum is obviously a labor of love for the two proprietors. And while not many people come through the doors on an average day, those that do will be entertained by their dialogues, their knowledge, and their perseverance in keeping the doors open. For me, personally, there were too many aviation toys from the "modern era," such as Hello Kitty, Barbie, Buzz Lightyear, Star Trek, and so on. But, as I was told, this is what today's kids want to see.

Having said that, older customers will enjoy hearing the stories of "Lindy, the New Flying Game," which came out after Lindbergh's famous flight, or the World War II–era "plane spotting "cards used for civil defense purposes on the home front, or even seeing the many "pot metal" toys, made out of junk metal in the 1930s, that were popular with the older generations.

This museum is one of the least visited museums in this book. It runs on the stringiest of shoestrings and is only open on weekends. But it is my sincere hope that others, readers like you, will find your way to this little corner storefront on Pritchard Street and check it out.

You will enjoy a brief visit here, and it will make these two very nice women quite happy.

The Nuts and Bolts

Top Fun Aviation Toy Museum
21 Pritchard Street
Fitchburg, Massachusetts 02140
(978) 342-2809
www.topfunaviation.com
This museum is handicapped accessible.

Travel Suggestion
The museum is located one block north of Main Street in downtown Fitchburg.

Museum Hours
Saturday, 10:30 a.m. to 4:30 p.m.;
Sunday, 1:30 p.m. to 4:30 p.m.

Admission
Regular admission is $5.00 for adults, which admits one child as well. Special rates for groups can be arranged.

Up around the Bend

The Aviation Toy Museum is located four blocks from the famous Fitchburg Art Museum. FAM is one of the area's most popular art museums and consists of four buildings and more than twenty thousand square feet of exhibit space. It first opened its doors in 1925.

REGION SIX
Pioneer Valley

Courtesy of Historic Deerfield.

33 Flynt Center of Early New England Life

~~~~~~

Deerfield

Like a Brigadoon rising out of the verdant Pioneer Valley of Massachusetts, Historic Deerfield is a magical place, seemingly frozen in time, forever preserved in amber and welcoming visitors to walk the footpaths of history to a time, some three centuries ago, that has been captured here in vivid still-life.

"The whole historic district is our museum," Laurie Nivison told me. She is the director of marketing. "We have a collection of twelve historic houses on a mile-long street. We actually consider the street to be an artifact in our collection. Each house was built between 1730 and 1850. Over time they have been filled with as near to original furnishings as possible. This area was a major crossroads of the Connecticut River Valley. Each year the river flooded mightily, and when the water retreated, it left behind some of the richest farming area in New England. So Deerfield had its share of wealthy citizens, and many of them owned these homes. Eleven of these homes are on the original plots where they were built."

Historic Deerfield is a living outdoor museum. In the fall, for example, when the New England colors are ablaze and giant pumpkins and cornstalks adorn each manicured front yard, visitors wander the quiet street entering each of the homes at a leisurely pace. Guides attend each building and can give family biographies and explanations of some of the priceless antiques that have made their way back here.

There are other buildings that comprise the historic district as well. "We have the Wilsons' Print Shop, in its original location. We have the Barnard Tavern and several others. And of course the Flynt Center," Nivison said.

"Henry and Helen Flynt of Greenwich, Connecticut, were the parents of a student attending Deerfield Academy, and they had expressed a keen interest in preserving the history of the town when they purchased their first house here in 1942. They later bought all the other historic houses we have today as they became available, and our Historic Deerfield was created. They were very generous and civic-minded. In addition to their interest in historic preservation, they also amassed a large collection of antiques, including, furniture, ceramics, silver, textiles, books, and more which are on display in the houses, in our library, and in the Flynt Center here today. They helped us obtain many of the antique furnishings and items we have here today. In 1952, they started the foundation from which Historic Deerfield sprang. Mrs. Flynt was an avid collector of early American textiles, and we have more than eight thousand pieces of textiles on site from her own collection," Nivison told me.

The second floor of the Flynt Center is called the "Museum's Attic." And that is basically what it is.

"Up here we have thousands of different items that we keep on display in what is considered 'visible storage' of the collection. We also have a large collection, parts of which we loan out to other museums and such. It really is like Deerfield's attic," she said as we slowly walked between gleaming, glass-enclosed display cases. The variety and quality of the items in "the attic" is astounding. Cases hold pieces of colonial furniture, valued at hundreds of thousands of dollars for each piece. Several cases hold countless pieces of expensive china. Others hold dozens of old cast-iron toys, as well as pieces of medical equipment, music boxes, hats, stoves and tea kettles, rifles, sewing tables, looking glasses, pewter tools, paintings, shaving brushes, hand-woven baskets, nutcrackers, bloodletting bowls, cigar-store Indians, clocks, and even a hand-carved wooden leg. "Our collection is very diverse as it shows the material culture of life in early America. At any given time we will have more than 2,500 items on display up here."

Wow Factor

"I do have a couple of pieces at the museum that I just cherish, but the wow factor for me involves a painting over here," Nivison remarked as we made our way through the crowd of visitors to a large painting on the wall. It is a fine oil portrait of an obviously wealthy woman. "The title of this painting is *Mary Jones*. It was painted by a western Massachusetts itinerant portrait artist, Erastus Salisbury Field, in 1836. As you can see, Mary is depicted in all of her elaborate finery of the day, including an expensive dress and an intricately hand-embroidered lace collar with flowers and a bobbin lace border."

The painting is indeed a wonderful piece of art, but to me, not unlike many of the colonial-era (and newer) portraits that we had seen throughout the museum.

"True," Nivison said. "But what makes this so special are two items that we can see in the portrait. Her fancy ring and her elaborate lace collar. Believe it or not, we actually have these items right here at the museum. What are the odds of that?" She pointed to Mary Jones's hand: "We have this ring in our collection. It is a beautiful copper ring made with gold alloy and studded with amethysts and garnets. Plus, as you can see, the most remarkably defined part of the portrait is her large, detailed lace collar. We have that too. From 1836. Amazing, isn't it?"

The Takeaway

What I liked most about Historic Deerfield is that there are equal parts indoors and outdoors to explore within the confines of this little historic district. The attic is a real surprise. I have never seen a collection of so many rare, historic rural antiques in a museum of this small size.

I was curious. How do they acquire these priceless items? Certainly the museum cannot have pockets that deep.

"Interesting that you ask," Nivison said. "Yes, some items literally walk in the door. But many times we are alerted to rare pieces of Old Deerfield that come up for auction around the country. Through the generous benevolence of some of our wealthy partners we have created a Collectors' Guild. These people, acting as a group, will come to our assistance when a rare piece comes up at auction, and they'll spring into action to acquire it for us. We simply couldn't complete our mission here without these wonderful people.

"In fact, the Collectors' Guild went into action on our behalf recently. In 2014, we learned that Sotheby's was going to feature an item that we absolutely knew came from one of our original twelve houses. It was a tall clock owned by Deerfield resident Asa Stebbins. A tall clock is also known as a grandfather clock, or longcase clock. We knew it was his because when Stebbins died in 1844, his probate papers, which we have, described an 'eight-day tall clock' which was affixed to the wall of the north parlor of his home right up the street from here. It was made in Boston and was valued at the time of his death at about fifteen dollars. Our Collectors' Guild engaged in the auction and purchased it for us for $185,000. It is breathtaking," she said.

"When the clock was returned to the Stebbins House across the street, we had a ceremony welcoming it home. The most remarkable thing is that when the historic engineers inspected the wall of the original parlor to see if it could still hold such a heavy item, they actually found the original holes in the wall where the clock had been placed nearly two centuries ago. The clock slid right into its old place on the parlor wall. It had finally come home," she observed quietly.

The Nuts and Bolts

Flynt Center of Early New England Life
(A Part of Historic Deerfield)
84B Old Main Street
Deerfield, Massachusetts 01342
(413) 774-5581
www.historic-deerfield.org/discover-deerfield/flynt
-center-of-early-new-england-life
This museum is handicapped accessible.

Travel Suggestion

This is the major visitor's attraction in Deerfield and the signage is excellent. You will have no trouble finding Historic Deerfield from either I-91 or Massachusetts Route 10. You can either park in the lot at the Flynt Center or out on the historic street. You should note that there are two museums within the borders of Historic Deerfield. The second one is called Memorial Hall Museum, owned by the Pocumtuck Valley Memorial Association. It actually predates Historic Deerfield.

Museum Hours

April through November: Daily, 9:30 a.m. to 4:30 p.m.; guided and self-guided tours are available.
December through March: Weekends, 9:30 a.m. to 4:30 p.m.

Admission

Adults: $18.00 ($7.00 in winter)
Children (6–17): $5.00
Ask about special off-season discounts.

Up around the Bend

There are three popular local businesses located just minutes from Historic Deerfield worth a visit. Richardson's Candy Kitchen is an old-fashioned candy store that has been making their own candy for decades and is known for their hand-dipped chocolates (www.richardsonscandy.com). The Old Deerfield Country Store (www.olddeerfieldcountrystore.com) is virtually next door to Richardson's and is a classic New England general store selling everything from lawn whirly-gigs to handy kitchen gadgets to holiday decorations. Both of these locations are just a few miles north of the home of the giant flagship store of Yankee Candle (www.yankeecandle.com/south-deerfield-village).

34 Westhampton Museum and Blacksmith Shop

Westhampton

"We really have no idea how many items there are in this museum," Barbara Pellissier, the president of the Westhampton Historical Society, admitted. "Certainly in the thousands of pieces."

The first section of this diminutive museum, tucked away in the Hidden Hills of western Massachusetts, is an original nineteenth-century blacksmith shop. These shops, which once were innumerable among the small towns and hamlets of the region, were critically important in the days of horse and wagons. "Yes, the blacksmith was usually the busiest man in town in those days," Pellissier told me. "And we like it that we can tell the story of the blacksmiths, and the whole mountain region, right here in such a historic little building."

The little red blacksmith shop holds a mind-numbing collection of rural Americana. A dozen pieces of vintage tin-smithing equipment, a hundred horseshoes (probably made right in this shop), and an uncountable number of original agricultural tools and implements that line the leaning walls of this old smithy.

"And we have a large collection of equipment that would have been used in this shop here also. Including some old hand-cranked forges. People from all over the mountains have contributed to our museum," she continued. There are two other newer buildings attached to the original blacksmith shop. They too are swallowed up in a snow globe of nostalgia. Perhaps the most unusual item, and maybe the rarest, is a large cabinet that contains the original town scale. Pellissier walked me over to it and opened the large double doors.

"As you can see this scale is absolutely complete. As such, it is extremely rare."

The scale, dating from 1915, was precise and calibrated routinely to measure precisely the items placed on its trays. An old sepia-colored chart tells how to measure quarts and pints and bushels and pecks. Customers would line up to have their goods weighed. I have never seen anything quite like this scale in all of the old buildings I have visited and researched around the countryside. With its intricate levers, gauges, scales, weights, and glossy wooden cabinet, it is a unique piece of nineteenth-century hardware.

The third part of the building, in the back, is referred to as the kitchen. Many old household items, again dating from the nineteenth century and earlier, are on display here. This room also contains hundreds of old black-and-white photographs from around the area. It is humbling to see these items from so long ago, representing as they do the hard work that went into almost every imaginable daily chore: washtubs, old press irons, maple syrup buckets and taps, intricate apple corers, woodenware, a cobbler's bench and tools, and much more.

Wow Factor

With all of the heavy, laborious, masculine work done in a blacksmith shop, I was most surprised at Pellissier's choice for a wow factor. "It is this little item right here," she said. She was holding a small, framed fabric sampler dated 1806. "Such a small, yet sweet and sentimental item this is. And it begs all who see it to conjure up the story behind it. We will never know for sure, of course, but we can imagine. We do know it was done by a nine-year-old girl named Almena Clark. As you can see the stitch work is exquisite. The numbers, letters, and images sewn into the cloth are just as clear today as they were when she completed it over two centuries ago. We have other samplers here in the museum, too. All young girls did them back in the day. But they are mostly faded and hard to decipher. This little one, however, is just destined to stay with us forever," she said.

I looked closely at the sampler, and it is stunning in its simplicity. The motto stitched across the front of it is poignant: "Virtue is a flower that never fades." From a nine-year-old, nonetheless. I did spy a little area of discoloring near the top of the sampler. I asked Pellissier about it.

"We don't know what that is but we suppose it is dried blood from where the little girl pricked her finger while creating this small, humble masterpiece."

Bob Dragon then accompanied us on our tour. Dragon has been around these parts forever and is currently on the Westhampton Historical Commission. I thought I would ask him for his wow factor also.

"Yessir, right here it is. A winter hearse," he said.

He showed me a large hearse on sleigh runners. The hearse was being "pulled" by a life-sized model of a horse. "I guess you could say that in the old days if you died in the winter and you were a long way from the cemetery, you got the last sleigh ride of your life right here on this winter hearse." The back of the hearse was taken over by a child's casket with a pane of glass in it. "It is a viewing casket," Dragon told me. "They are rare, yes, but as for the winter hearse, well, sir, we have never seen one like this before."

The Takeaway

We have all seen and visited museums like this one. Small buildings just crammed with dusty, old-timey things that sit on the floors and shelves bearing silent witness to the daily goings on of three, four, and five generations ago. I have visited dozens of these rural reposi- tories. But this one was unusually interesting. It is only open one day a week (Sunday) so normally some representative of the historical society will be at the museum to share stories with you. The natural placement of this blacksmith shop is beautiful, high on a hill with just a couple of two-hundred-year-old buildings as its neighbors.

If I had to choose a word to describe my visit to the Blacksmith Museum, I would say "pleasant." Nice people, unusual items, and great stories from the past.

One last note. As you walk up the path to the museum, you will see a giant, black polished anvil with the name "Pomeroy" carved across the top. The Pomeroys were one of the founding families of the Hidden Hills region of Massachusetts, and they came to America around 1630. They were blacksmiths. The monument mentions the earliest Pomeroy settlers of the area, with great old first names like Ebenezer, Deacon, Eltweed, Pliny, and Thankful. Their original fam- ily anvil was given to Medad Pomeroy by the town of Northampton in 1660. Today, that anvil is in the museum there.

A descendant of the Pomeroy family found the anvil in the museum one day and has set out to recreate it at many places important to the Pomeroy family in America over the centuries. The Pomeroy Anvil Trail now consists of a dozen of these giant anvils across the country, each one telling of the family's history as pertains to that region. The five-by-eight-foot-tall, six-ton black granite monument was placed here most fittingly at the Blacksmith Museum in 2007, by William Guilford Pomeroy, Jr., the fourth great-grandson of Pliny Pomeroy.

The Nuts and Bolts

Westhampton Museum and Blacksmith Shop

5 Stage Road
Westhampton, Massachusetts 01207
(413) 527-1731
https://pvhn.wordpress.com/locations/westhampton
-blacksmith-shop-museum/
The museum building is a little dark and very crowded; it might not be convenient for those with mobility issues.

Travel Suggestion

Do not get confused. Westhampton is west of Northampton, north of Southampton, and northwest of Easthampton. Like I said, don't get confused!

Museum Hours

Memorial Day to mid-October: Sundays, 2 p.m. to 4 p.m. They end their season with a large fall festival.

Admission

Free

Up around the Bend

Westfield is located fifteen miles south of this museum. This village was known as the "Whip Capital of the World" at one time. There is one surviving whip-maker left, the Westfield Whip Manufacturing Company, and it is housed in its original 1887 brick factory building.

Photograph by Kevin Rutherford. Creative Commons license available at: https://creativecommons.org/licenses/by-sa/4.0/.

35 Calvin Coolidge Presidential Library and Museum

Northampton

This is the only presidential museum and library actually located *inside a public library.*

"We are very proud of Mr. Coolidge, and it is an honor to tell his story here. Just because his personality was reserved doesn't mean that his administration, in fact his whole life, doesn't warrant a respectful review by the general public," said Julie Nelson, archivist of the Calvin Coolidge Presidential Library.

I asked her, "Why Northampton?"

"Calvin Coolidge was born in Vermont, but he attended schools here in Massachusetts and, in fact, he spent his entire political life here until he became president. He started in the lower offices but was quickly noticed, became a well-known and respected administrator, and found himself to be popular with voters. Coolidge was elected clerk of the courts, Massachusetts state representative, two-term mayor of Northampton, four terms in the Massachusetts state senate, lieutenant governor, and then finally was elected the forty-eighth governor of the state in 1918.

"It was said that Coolidge had the magic touch with the voters. He ran for political office on many occasions and always won. Except once. And that has an interesting story to it."

I asked the archivist about it.

"It seems that in 1905, Mr. Coolidge ran for the Northampton City School Board. It was a close election, but he lost. A group of his friends later told him that they had heard he lost because he had no children of his own and some thought he would not be able to relate to children's educational issues. His reply was pure Calvin Coolidge. 'No kids? I was just married, give me time.'"

How did the future president take his sole loss at the ballot box?

"Well, he was determined to never have that happen again," she said. "In fact, and this is true, exactly one year and one day after his schoolboard loss, Mrs. Coolidge gave birth to their first child, John Calvin."

The museum can be found in a large room on the second floor of the Forbes Free Public Library across the street from Smith College in downtown Northampton. It consists of display cases breaking down the eras of the Calvin Coolidge timeline (The Boston Years, The Presidential Years, etc.) and memorabilia from his extensive political career, including archival photographs, furniture, campaign novelties, and artwork.

"People forget that before Franklin D. Roosevelt, presidential papers, records, and historical items belonged to the presidents themselves and literally could, and did, end up scattered across the country after they left Washington. Now, of course, each president has his own large library, and they have become major tourist destinations," Nelson told me. "Not so in Coolidge's day. In fact, the day after his administration ended, seven large U.S. Army trucks departed the White House loaded down with the Coolidges' archives, papers, and personal property. Four of them were directed here to the Forbes Library, one of them went directly to the Coolidge residence in Northampton, and another one was taken to a secret bank vault."

Wow Factor

Although perhaps the smallest presidential library in the country, there are a surprising number of unusual items here that certainly meet the "wow" standard. "Well, I have three wow factors, actually," she told me. "It is hard to say what is my favorite, so let me tell you about all of them."

Nelson took me over to an eye-catching, tall glass exhibit case. The item inside was instantly recognizable.

"One of the most famous photographs ever taken of any president was taken of President Coolidge in August of 1927. His administration had pushed for many changes in the way that Native Americans were treated. In fact, he advocated for full citizenship for Native American veterans, which was controversial at the time. He signed the Indian Citizenship Act of 1924. To honor him, many Native American tribes welcomed him to their regions during his summer travels in 1927. In Deadwood, South Dakota, he was presented a full, floor-length Sioux feather headdress. The photo of him wearing it, all the while dressed in his three-piece, high-collar business suit, made for great laughs. But I love it, and we have the headdress here."

The Indian headdress is magnificent. Hundreds of beads and feathers cascade down from the top to the sweeping "tail," which rests just above the floor. I, like most everyone who loves presidential history, have seen this headdress in that famous photograph before, and I couldn't help but smile at the idea of it standing in front of me.

"Another wow factor for me is the electric riding horse over here," she pointed. Looking all the world like a modern day rodeo bronco-busting *Urban Cowboy* mechanical bull, this contraption stands five feet tall, is made out of black solid steel, and weighs 350 pounds. "It is an odd piece I have to admit," she smiled. "But Mr. Coolidge loved to ride horses, and his availability to do that in Washington was, shall we say, rather limited. So Dr. John Harvey Kellogg presented this electric horse to the president. Kellogg, who invented the corn flake, also had a keen interest in health and wellness and thought that this piece of equipment would both stimulate and relax the president during his stay within the confines of the White House. Any kid who visits here comes right over to see this. This is also the item most requested to go on loan from this museum. In fact, they have even had it on display at the Kentucky Derby and at the Gene Autry Museum."

And her last wow factor?

"These two beautiful portraits," she said as she pointed to a large wall. "They were done by one of the most famous artists of his time, Howard Chandler Christy. The portraits of Mr. and Mrs. Coolidge actually hung in the White House during his term of office, but they were brought here to Northampton after the Coolidges left Washington. As you can see they are very large, and Mr. Christy purposely painted them so they could be positioned next to each other, as if Calvin and his wife, Grace, were looking at each other. And that is the way they were installed here, although we did not have a place to hang them at first. The building architects created this entire wall just so these two paintings could be hung here as the artist had planned."

They are beautiful, especially the luminous portrayal of Grace Coolidge.

"Yes, she was a beautiful woman. There is a much more famous Christy painting of Mrs. Coolidge in the White House today. He painted it in 1924. It is a stunning portrayal of the First Lady in a flaming red 'flapper dress' posing with her large white collie dog, Rob Roy. It hangs in the formal China Room in the White House and has been called one of the most beautiful of all the First Lady official portraits."

The Takeaway

There is much to be learned about the "accidental president," Calvin Coolidge, in this one-room presidential library. He was a complex man, a natural introvert who preferred to be on the sidelines, a public servant who always lived in private homes, stayed in no governor's mansion, and was not totally at ease in the public limelight.

"He lived here in Northampton during his time as governor. He would take the train into Boston on Monday and come back home to his family on Friday night.

"I think the public perception of President Coolidge really does not match up to the actual makeup of the man," Nelson said. "He was thrust into the White House upon the death of his predecessor, Warren G. Harding. He was an innovative thinker who lived in progressive times. His personality, at the dawning of film and radio, didn't quite lend itself to the new mediums naturally."

I asked Nelson about the sobriquet "Silent Cal."

"Ah, yes, Silent Cal," she smiled. "Well, he was a man of few words, but we believe there might be a dark side to that nickname. His youngest son, also named Calvin, died at just sixteen years old. He acquired a blister on his foot while playing tennis, which quickly grew to be infected and ultimately caused his death. It was a major shock to everybody. For a time, many believed incorrectly that he got the infection because he wore black socks while playing tennis and that the dye in them had infected him. In fact, black socks were actually banned after the president's son's death, and that is why we have white socks for tennis attire today. Those that knew him well sensed that President Coolidge went into a deep depression after his son's untimely death, a depression which he battled perhaps for the rest of his life. And that may have contributed to his quiet, insular persona. We just don't know. We do know that President Coolidge had a very short retirement period after his presidency. He died at the age of only sixty."

The Nuts and Bolts

Calvin Coolidge Presidential Library and Museum

20 West Street
Northampton, Massachusetts 01060
(413) 587-1014
www.forbeslibrary.org/calvin-coolidge-presidential
-library-and-museum
This museum is handicapped accessible.

Travel Suggestion

The museum is located on the second floor of the Forbes Library, near the entrance to Smith College. It is about one block away from the bustling downtown business district of Northampton.

Museum Hours

Mondays, 9 a.m. to 5 p.m.; Tuesdays, 1 p.m. to 5 p.m.; Wednesdays, 4 p.m. to 9 p.m.; Thursdays, 1 p.m. to 5 p.m.

Admission

Free

Up around the Bend

A weekend's worth of adventures could be scheduled for a visit to this lovely college community. There are several arts centers, galleries, outdoor recreation activities, and live performance venues scattered all over this city of nearly thirty thousand. A good starting point to craft your custom weekend here is to visit www.explorenorthampton.com.

36 Noble and Cooley Center for Historic Preservation

Granville

The first impression one gets when driving up to the massive, wooden campus of buildings that makes up the Noble & Cooley Drum Company in tiny Granville is how sprawling this business really is. Huge old wooden buildings, some three and four stories tall, some even connected by a skyway bridge for workers to go from one building to the next, fill the landscape off a dirt road and completely surrounded by lush, wooded acres. You think to yourself, "How many workers must there be inside making drums?"

"Three. Just the three of us," Jay Jones told me. He is the president of Noble & Cooley, and he was referring to himself, his wife, Carol, and their son, Nick. "The company has been open since 1854, and we have turned out toy drums every year of our existence. We started making toy drums but now we mostly make high-end drums for professional musicians around the world. We have even made drums that have been used in rock and roll tours.

"Anybody I would have heard of before?" I asked.

"Paul McCartney. Phil Collins. Want more names? Are they good enough for you?" he laughed.

Jay Jones is a friendly, easy-going guy with an enormous legacy on his shoulders. His family started this company in 1854. "That's the founder right there," he said, pointing to a portrait on his office wall. "James P. Cooley. Four greats ago," he continued, with a proud smile. "I am sixth generation. And when it is time for me to hang it up, my son Nick will take it to the seventh. And that little guy running around over there is Jack, my grandson. He doesn't know it yet, but he is number eight."

We began our walk through the historic buildings, floor after floor and department after department. Along the way, the owner described the art of drum-making to me, the story of his family's connection to the industry, as well as some of the fantastic history held within the walls of these ancient structures.

As we climbed a set of creaky old stairs, we came to the museum floor. Here is where the history lives. And it is significant.

"We didn't just make drums, we made history here. Can you imagine that we used to have 120 workers here turning out thousands of drums a week. We have a ledger that shows we produced 631 drums in 1854. In 1873, that number was up to 80,000. During the Civil War we made hundreds of drums for the Union Army. We even made a drum for Abraham Lincoln. It was used during his presidential campaign. Our company went to Illinois and procured a rail post from a fence that had actually been split by Lincoln. When it arrived here it was used for the basis of a drum for him. It was a showpiece. We bent the split-rail fence post, adorned it with silver hooks, silk cords, and had a likeness of Lincoln painted on the head of the drum. If you look over here, you can see that my great-great-great-grandfather was mighty proud of his work."

With that, Jones pointed to a diary entry made by James P. Cooley. It was dated August 18, 1860, and read, "Finished the Lincoln drum today, the finest thing ever made." In a testament to Mr. Cooley's Yankee sensibility, he ended the diary notation with this: "Also got in the wheat, 175 sheaves."

I asked Jones about the museum, which is relatively new. "A few years back we hosted a tour for the Society of Industrial Archeologists, a prestigious group of history preservationists. We demonstrated the veneering, the steam bending, and even ran the eight-color press for them. Their jaws dropped to the floor when they saw what we had here, and they impressed upon us that we simply had to organize a museum to make it available for the public to see."

I asked him what in particular caught their eye.

"Well, in the old days, whenever our company needed a new machine to make a part or something, we simply made it ourselves. Nobody had anything we needed, so our machinists created all of our own machines. And we still have them. They are unique to the business and are one-of-a-kind historic artifacts. The folks in the tour could not believe their eyes. They asked how we kept our competitors' 'roving eyes' away from these creations. I told them, our owners never acquired a patent on anything they made. They didn't want others to look up the patent specifications and try to make their own machines like ours."

"So they really kept it a secret?" I opined.

"Yes, for example, the printing press was kept in a locked room where only the pressmen and the owners were allowed in. Nobody outside of these walls ever saw these machines. The secret was safe. Kind of simple, really. But it worked."

While the story of the Lincoln campaign drum is certainly a story to stir one's pride, it is another drum that levels your mood. "We made a drum for Lincoln's funeral, too. It is still around and is in private hands. *Smithsonian Magazine* recently did a story on Lincoln's assassination. One of the drums played at the president's funeral was a Noble & Cooley. It still has some of the original black bunting that was put on it for the funeral." He showed me the photograph.

"Now that is history," he said.

Wow Factor

The fact that they made so many drums here during the Civil War is one thing, but to actually have one of them is rare. They have one here, and it is Jones's wow factor.

"As you can see it is a large drum," he began as we looked into a large glass display case. The drum was certainly aged and worn but still retained a remarkable sense of purpose and dignity to it. "It is in excellent condition, which is very unusual for the era. This drum was picked up off the battlefield at Gettysburg by a soldier in the Pennsylvania Company F28 (he had been a musician in the 131st before transferring), and he simply took it home with him. It stayed in that person's family for generations until we acquired it. It features leather 'ears,' which were used to tune it, and was made out of oak and tulip wood. The drum head was made out of calfskin. The drum still has the Noble & Cooley maker's mark inside the drum. When you think about the incredible history and importance of the Battle of Gettysburg, and then realize that some young man was marching onto the bloody battlefield beating one our drums, well, that is pretty special to all of us here."

The Takeaway

I had goosebumps throughout my personal tour of this museum. One epic piece of history after another kept leaping out at me from the text, the photographs, or the display cases scattered around the old factory floor.

When I first pulled into the parking area of the factory, I looked up and saw a curious sight. A gigantic drum was perched at the peak of the roof. The drum, and the eagle weathervane on top of it, was placed there in 1889. I mentioned to Jones that whoever put that drum up there must have had quite a view of the surrounding area.

"Want to see it for yourself?" he asked.

I couldn't say yes fast enough. I followed him as we threaded our way up and up and up through abandoned rooms until we reached a small ladder. Once "into" the drum you can see that the head is made out of dazzling, old stained glass. The view from this unusual aerie was fantastic.

I give Jones and his small family so much credit for keeping this incredible slice of Americana alive and going despite hardships and economic downturns. He got quite emotional talking about his role as the family standard-bearer into the future.

"I cannot leave this place. I am too old to go anywhere and too young to retire. So we stay in this gigantic eighty-thousand-square-foot factory and make as many drums as we can. Each one is a work of art. Each drum we make is touched by our hands. But I will never leave. I walk through the old shops and buildings here and I run into my dad and my grandfathers and all of the ghosts of those who came before me. This is me. This is my history."

Jay, Carol, and Nick Jones are heroes in my eyes.

The Nuts and Bolts

Noble and Cooley Center for Historic Preservation

Located within the Noble & Cooley Factory buildings
42 Water Street
Granville, Massachusetts 01034
(413) 357-6321
www.ncchp.org
Parts of this museum are handicapped accessible.

Travel Suggestion

Although this is a very sparsely populated area, and Granville is just a three-corner intersection of roads, the signage to the museum is good.

Museum Hours

This museum is open by appointment or from noon to 3 p.m. on the second and fourth Sundays of the month, May through November.

Admission

Adults: $5.00
Children: $3.00
Note: When calling in advance, be sure and ask if Jay Jones will be there. He is most willing to take groups, large or small, on a guided tour of the museum. There is also a small gift shop that sells toys, hand-carved local objects, and, of course, toy drums made right here at the factory.

Up around the Bend

One of the only businesses in Granville is the Granville Country Store. This little store sells many unique food items, none as famous as their own Granville Cellar Aged Cheddar. This cheese has been made and stored in the cellar of the store since 1851. It is now sold in many larger stores and online. I would recommend that you stop here and buy this great, tangy-tasting cheddar cheese right where it has been made for over 150 years.

37 Chester Railway Station Museum

～⌐

Chester

There are several things that Massachusetts has an embarrassing amount of. Like famous birthplaces. And Revolutionary War landmarks. And restaurants serving chowder.

And railroad museums.

I really wanted to feature a railroad museum in this book. But which one? There are plenty to choose from, and they offer a wide variety of amenities for the visitor to experience. Old station houses and depots restored to the glory days of the rails. Actual rides on old steamers and passenger trains. Artifacts and displays of valuable memorabilia, uniforms, equipment, and ephemera unique to each rail line. So which historic railroad would it be to represent all of the wonderful ones in the Bay State?

Surely the Berkshire Scenic Railway Museum in Lenox would

have to be considered. It is perhaps the most popular of them all. Or the quaint and little known Old Colony and Fall River Railroad Museum, located almost directly under the guns of the USS *Massachusetts* at Battleship Cove in Fall River. That is one of the least-visited railroad museums in the state. I've taken a ride on the small Cape Cod Central Railroad, and it is charming. A two-hour narrated ride, originating in Hyannis, rolling past marshes, cranberry bogs, and canals. These, and many others, are all great choices. But I wanted one that would be a little more out of the way, under the radar, and off the beaten path.

And that path took me to little Chester, in Hampden County. And it also took me to Dave Pierce's doorstep. He is the president of the museum and the Chester Foundation.

"Yup, I live right across the street," Pierce laughed as he pointed to a red house literally at the foot of the driveway to the museum. "I guess you could say I am kind of the overseer of the whole place."

That "place" is the Chester Railway Station Museum, an active set of Amtrak and CSX rails that run right behind it, and several old railroad cars on the front lawn of the depot.

Let's start with the train cars.

"Well, sir, that over there is 1930 Vulcan steam locomotive built in Wilkes-Barre, Pennsylvania. When we got it, it was working the Deer Island Granite Quarry in Maine," he said as we walked around a locomotive that looked exactly as we might have imagined it to look from that era. The colors were freshly painted in black, silver, and bright red; the tall steam smokestack loomed above it all; an open-air conductor's cab was perched right behind the wheels. "And that one over there is a 1919 railroad caboose from the Rutland Railroad in Vermont. And the other one, well that one is the real eye-catcher of them all."

He was speaking of the Baker's Chocolate train car. "That carried chocolate ingredients, wax, syrup, all kinds of stuff. Ours carried mostly wax. It was not an original and was black when we got it. We painted the Baker's logo on it to liven it up. It is one of the most famous logos in train history, and the Baker's Chocolate cars ended up being made into a series of popular model trains."

This large tanker car is painted white so it sticks out from all the other black tank cars you would see going by at a railroad crossing. The logo is of a woman in a large dress and apron serving up hot chocolate. It is believed that this logo is the oldest registered trademark in America.

"Everybody knows that image. It is from a famous 1743 painting called *La Belle Chocolatiere* ('The Chocolate Girl'). Because of the white tank car and the image of the girl with the hot chocolate, it was recreated on thousands of little model cars. We have a display of those inside, and almost every gauge of the toy train cars made, we have it: G, O, S, HO, and N. You don't see that very often."

As we moved to the station entrance I commented on how beautiful, how graceful the depot was architecturally.

"Not many know this, but the architect was George Washington Whistler, one of the chief design engineers for the Western Railroad. He built many stations, although very few are left. They are all aesthetically pleasing to the eye. The Italianate design of ours features fanciful ironwork, post-and-beam construction, the use of gleaming American chestnut wood for the interior, and tall sunlight-catching windows. We added the railings because in its original location they weren't needed. There are only three timber-frame stations like this left—ours, one that has been turned into a residence, and one that is used as a mechanic's garage. Despite all of that, people still find that the biggest curiosity here is the backstory about the architect himself."

"And that story would be?" I asked.

"George Washington Whistler was a very famous man. He was a canal and lock engineer of national repute and had his hand in the construction of several famous American railroads. The Western was the most famous because of all the many superlatives and innovations. At the time, Whistler was responsible for many hundreds of miles of New England railroad. In fact, his fame led him to building the first Russian railroad from Moscow to St. Petersburg. Still, despite all of this, his wife, Anna, was even more famous."

"Let me guess," I smiled.

"Yes, she was 'Whistler's Mother,' the subject of one of the most famous paintings in the world. George Washington Whistler's son, James, was the artist."

Inside the Chester depot we find numerous tall glass exhibit cases packed with railroadiana. Photographs, lanterns, tools, uniforms, schedules and tickets, conductor badges, old phones, station furniture, menus, mailbags, and too many more items to recount. Unusual items that struck me included an actual two-foot-wide front headlamp from a locomotive, some sledge hammers from the days of the railroad's construction ("Go ahead, pick it up," Pierce told me. I did, and I would not want to be swinging that all day long in the sun), and a striking, colorful scale model overhead view of the valley and the railroad threading through it.

"I made that myself," he said proudly. It might appear at first that Dave Pierce is a one-man show at this museum. Not so. "We have a number of excellent board members who all bring special talents that allow this station to thrive. Most of our revenue is generated now by being an event venue. We have people who put in many valuable hours in this museum, serving as a matter of civic pride."

"But, yes, I'm the one that is here most of the time. I have had a love of the railroad most of my life, and I slowly got involved here. Of course, it helps that I live across the street. I watch for people to pull up, and I will come over and give them tours. It is real history, right here in our little town, and I am thankful to be a part of it."

Wow Factor

"Let's go back outside and I will show you," Pierce said when I asked him for his wow factor.

"It would have to be the caboose. It was built in 1919, and when we found it, it had been sitting in a field in Agawam. It was in pretty rough shape, but we knew we had to have it for our museum. It has a conductor's cupola on top. We had to remove that in order to get it here to this location. There is a small stone tunnel at the end of our road, and the caboose was too tall with the cupola on it."

I asked Pierce how he remedied that problem.

"Simple, we just took it off and attached it to a guy's little Toyota pickup truck and drove it here, all the while hoping we wouldn't be stopped by the police," he laughed. There is a photo album of the whole move, including original photos of the caboose in the field as well as the detached cupola strapped precariously to the roof rack of the Toyota.

The inside of the caboose has been refurbished to as close to original as possible. "It was a lot of hard work, but we are pretty proud of how it came out. It has a conductor's office where he would go and sit at his desk to fill out the paperwork. The raised cupola has of course been reattached, and you can see it fits four trainmen comfortably. From this high location they kept their eyes open for trouble from fires, hobos, equipment malfunctions, or whatever. These guys could sense trouble from up here, and they were ready to act. If not, they just watched for trains coming from the other direction and would wave as their fellow trainmen passed by in their own caboose. They were always watching out for each other, scanning for shifting loads or dragging equipment."

This is a remarkable car. The wood is in great shape, and the seats are comfortable. There is an old one-holer bathroom, which is not in use, and a pot-belly stove. A barrel of the last coal shoveled into the stove is still in the caboose.

"We actually rent this caboose out for overnight groups. They really enjoy it. Scout groups, youth groups, and all sorts of people stay here for the thrill of it all. We bring out camp fire material for them and some picnic tables. And, of course, we let them use the bathrooms inside the museum."

The Takeaway

The whole museum is a bit unassuming. But with Dave Pierce or others from the museum staff at your side, you can begin to imagine the importance and significance of this rural rail station.

"A journalist once wrote that our part of the state was the worst possible place in the world you should ever dream of building a railroad. Another said it would be as useless as building a railroad to the moon. Our area is high, rough, and covered with forests. Because of our railroad, what once was an eight-day stagecoach ride was shortened to an eight-hour train ride. But it was tough. The workers had to hand-cut twenty-one bridges in just one twelve-mile section. Still, at one time we had the longest bridge in the world (1,258 feet spanning the Connecticut River), the highest railroad in the world, and the first American railroad built by a large mass of immigrants (3,000 Irish workers).

The Nuts and Bolts

Chester Railway Station Museum

10 Prospect Street
Chester, Massachusetts 01011
(413) 354-7878
www.chesterrailwaystation.net
This museum is handicapped accessible.

Travel Suggestion

While driving down the small Main Street you can see
the station on the other side of the tunnel underpass.

Museum Hours

July through September: Saturday to Tuesday, 11 a.m.
to 3 p.m.
Visits at other times are by appointment, but
Dave Pierce will come over if he sees you arrive.

Admission

Free but donations are encouraged.

Up around the Bend

The Keystone Arches are a series of famous stone railroad arches
located just up the road from the museum. Ask at the depot for
hiking instructions. These arches are nationally famous and they
made possible the whole history of the Western Railroad. They
are beautiful.

38 The *Titanic* Museum

Indian Orchard

It is hard to imagine that the story of the RMS *Titanic* was ever not an epic news story.

"Sure it was very big news when it first happened," Karen Kamuda told me. She is the owner of the *Titanic* Museum in this Springfield suburb. "But the hoopla died down real quick as World War I took over the headlines. There was no twenty-four-hour cable news service, of course, so after the initial shock dissipated, the sinking of the *Titanic* kind of moved off the front pages and into the background. As recently as the early 1950s, there were many survivors of the 1912 disaster still alive, but they were forgotten and nobody really was interested in their stories."

Kamuda's late husband Ed was the driving force behind the museum.

"Ed just could not get enough of the *Titanic* story. When he was a kid, his grandfather showed the 1953 movie *Titanic* right across the street in the Grand Theater, which was family-owned. The movie, which starred Barbara Stanwyck and Clifton Webb, was produced by the J. Arthur Rank Organization in the United Kingdom. The Rank group had little confidence in American theaters showing this film properly, so they sent along a promotional kit to help theater owners hype the film and draw in large audiences. At the time, there were around eighty-seven *Titanic* survivors living in the UK, Canada, and the U.S. Rank sent along a list of all of their names and addresses suggesting that movie houses invite them to come and make a personal appearance at the film's showing to draw attention to it. Well, Ed, who was only fourteen at the time, got that list from his grandfather, and he personally wrote to all eighty-seven of them asking about their stories. Unbelievably, seventy-five sent letters back to Ed. From then on he was hooked."

The *Titanic* Museum is located in a large back section of a jewelry store that is owned by Ed's sister, Barbara Kamuda. Karen manages the museum. It consists of two large rooms with glass display cases filled with *Titanic* memorabilia. There are photographs of virtually anything and everything that had to do with the ship's sinking, from images of the *Titanic* itself to pictures of the rescue ships, photographs of the passengers, maps, and movie posters, plus a small library of *Titanic* books. Larger pieces of memorabilia are scattered around both rooms. A large model of the ship, meticulous in its detail, sits near the entrance from the jewelry store to the museum.

"We try and display as many items as we can here in this little museum. But some of our premier items are on loan to various museums and historical sites. There are two large *Titanic* museums, one in Branson, Missouri, and another in Pigeon Forge, Tennessee. We have several items on display that we have loaned both venues. One of our most prized artifacts is in the museum in Branson. It is one of only three known cork life preservers to survive from the doomed ship.

And ours actually belonged to Madeline Astor, the pregnant teenage bride of one of the richest men in the world, John Jacob Astor IV. Mr. Astor went down with the ship, and Mrs. Astor survived, no doubt because of the vest she wore and which we now own," Kamuda said.

The museum in Indian Orchard has plenty of *Titanic* memories to share, all cluttered around large models of the rescue ships, ship accoutrements like bells and flags, silverware, pieces of the ship's carpeting, and even a bread board from the *Titanic*'s kitchen.

Kamuda, who is usually on hand to give an in-depth narrative of the ship, its fate, and the museum's contents, is an expert without parallel on this subject. And she is quite a storyteller to boot.

Wow Factor

"It is not much, but I think it is extra special," Kamuda said as we peered into a large glass display case. The object of our attention was a small pocket watch.

"It belonged to Milton Clyde Long, who was a native of Springfield. He was only just a young man when he died in the sinking of the ship. He was the son of a former mayor of Springfield. We think he jumped from the *Titanic* just as it went under. Years later his family would periodically bring the watch in for repairs, and our family (who owned the jewelry store) never knew of the connection. Once we found out it belonged to young Milton, we acquired it. It is just so poignant to have this watch of his, a native of our hometown who died in the tragedy."

The Takeaway

As much as I enjoyed hearing all the backstories to the items on display at the museum, I felt that the real story was the connection of this place to the blockbuster James Cameron film *Titanic* (1997). It is an incredible story.

"James Cameron has been in our museum several times, and he stays in touch with us," Kamuda said. "Cameron conferred many times with my husband Ed about certain aspects of the ship he recreated for his film. He wanted it to be just right. It was known that Ed was the 'go-to source' for everything *Titanic*. In fact, Ed worked closely with Dr. Robert Ballard in identifying the wreckage of the *Titanic* when Ballard and his team found it on the ocean floor in 1985.

"The movie director created a painstaking replica of the great ship for the epic film. He even invited my husband and me to go and see it. It was on a giant set in Rosarito Beach, Mexico. James Cameron flew us down and took us to the ship's set personally. It was unforgettable."

I asked her how Ed felt being on the ship.

"When we emerged from the inside of the ship and stepped out on the polished wooden well deck, it was really too much for my husband. He got very emotional. He looked up at the towering four smokestacks and said, 'Oh, my God.' He had been studying this ship since he was a kid and to be on something about as close to the real thing as you can get, well, it was the high point of my late husband's life and career for sure."

"How did you feel about the whole experience?" I asked Karen.

"It was wonderful of course. But what I really enjoyed was being in the movie," she laughed. "James Cameron honored us by allowing Ed and me to be extras in the cast of the movie. It was so fun," she said as she showed me some movie stills from the film showing the couple, all gussied up in Victorian-era clothes, in the background of a scene with Leonardo DiCaprio and Kathy Bates.

The Nuts and Bolts

The *Titanic* Museum
208 Main Street
Indian Orchard, Massachusetts 01151
(413) 543-4770
www.titanichistoricalsociety.org/museum
This museum is handicapped accessible.

Travel Suggestion
There is literally no outdoor sign for this museum, so look for it by street address. Keep your eye out for Henry's Jewelry Store. That is it! There is a small blue notice on the inside of the store window telling you of the museum in the back.

Museum Hours
Monday through Friday, 10 a.m. to 4 p.m.; Saturday, 10 a.m. to 3 p.m. Closed holidays.

Admission
Adults: $4.00
Children under 12: $2.00

Up around the Bend

Just about six miles from Indian Orchard is Springfield, the birthplace of Dr. Seuss (Theodor Geisel). A whimsical National Memorial Sculpture Garden located at the Springfield Museums depicts many of Seuss's favorite characters in bronze, from Horton (hearing his Who) to The Grinch and his little dog Max, to the Cat (definitely in his Hat) and the diminutive Lorax.

REGION SEVEN
Berkshires

39 Susan B. Anthony Birthplace Museum

~~~~~~~~

Adams

Long before she was a leading force of nature in the women's rights movement, Susan B. Anthony was just a little girl living in this modest, federal-style home on the hilly outskirts of Adams.

"Susan only lived here until she was six years old, but this is where her moral compass was set," Colleen Janz, executive director of this museum, told me. "In this house, she was surrounded by dominating women whose forceful personalities set the course for Susan's own pioneering work. Her parents, Daniel and Lucy, created quite a stir when they entered a (then) forbidden marriage between a Quaker man and a Baptist woman. Lucy was a powerful influence on little Susan and quite a character in her own right. Shockingly, she even wore red dresses," Janz told me.

This house is small and compact yet at one time held quite a contingent of family members and mill workers. "Susan's father owned a mill across the road," Janz continued. "At times, he let his workers live in the upstairs rooms. These workers, mostly young women, worked the looms at the mill. Once there were eleven of the twenty-two workers living upstairs in the attic, all young women who stayed in the attic sharing mattresses made of horsehair and hay, which were then wrapped in fabric."

The first floor of the house consists of a kitchen, parlor, living area, and bedroom. The front northerly corner of the house was set up as her father's store. He sold products from the mill such as broadcloth, buckets of lime for gardening and other uses, and other necessities. He also sold booze. It was hard cider at first. "Daniel Anthony had a long history as what we would call today being a 'rum runner.' Several times he got called on this endeavor both by the locals and by his Quaker brethren. In order for Daniel to sell liquor, hard cider, and rum, he had to appease the church by agreeing to never sell to Quakers, to use consignments so that he wasn't using his own money, and that he would have to increase his tithe to match a portion of his proceeds from the liquor sales. In addition, he allowed women to sell their wares, from baked goods to eggs to sewn items from their kitchens. As women were considered property, they could not just buy and sell products without the transactions going through their husbands first. To get around that, Daniel allowed the women to earn 'points' rather than money. The points could then be used to purchase material from his mill or other women's products."

Eventually, chafing at all of this close observation by his neighbors, Daniel set out to chase a more lucrative financial future in Battenville, located in Washington County in northern New York. I asked the director if that was a move that went over well with Susan, then just a tyke who presumably was settled in her home with her young friends and neighbors nearby.

"No," was the emphatic answer. "Susan was a feisty youngster, having learned at the feet of several strong-willed women, including her own mother and grandmothers. In fact, Susan's response to her father's declaration of the impending move was recorded at the time. It is said that Susan pitched a fit, threw a heroic temper tantrum, and went thundering up the stairs to her bedroom in a screaming fury. Meanwhile, her family retired to the dining room to have supper. Once in her room she continued her tiny tempest by pounding and stomping on the floorboards so hard that the dust from ceiling lath plaster fell down and into her father's stew bowl."

Wow Factor

"I am partial to one room in particular," Janz said. We walked into the "birthing room" and stood at the foot of a large bed. "This room still gives me goose bumps. This is the actual room where Susan B. Anthony was born on February 15, 1820. It was a cold and bitter night, and luxuries were few. Susan's grandmother was the midwife. Delivery was an excruciating experience then, and in fact delivery was the leading cause of death at the time. But despite all of this, Susan arrived. To think that through all of that anxiousness and pain a young life was created. A life that changed the world. I just find being in this room so important and emotional."

A personal wow factor of my own is a bust of Anthony's head. "This is wonderful," Janz said. "She visited a phrenologist when she was thirty-three. He was a scientist who correlated brain size with different functions. He was quite amazed at what he discovered about her, and we have a statement from him framed on the wall above the head."

The first line said in so many words the totality of the personality that we have come to know from her: "You are a woman who always works with a will, a purpose and a straightforwardness of mental action."

Janz observed, "When young people come through the museum we invite them to run their own hands over 'Susan's head,' so they can experience what the phrenologist was looking for. They love it."

The Takeaway

Susan B. Anthony lived in several homes located around the Northeast including three in New York State—Battenville (now Greenwich), Canajoharie (demolished), and Rochester. Each existing home tells of the different stage of life she was going through at that particular time. But this house is special because it tells the story of how Anthony was molded, her earliest influences, and the impetus for her drive for independence, both in her own personal life and for women in general. The house is charming, the exhibits are well-displayed and attractive, and there is much information to be garnered from a visit here.

The dining room is now called the Legacy Room, and it has an abundance of information about Susan's life and times, all well-thought-out through text, images, and timelines. The great names of the era leap off the walls, such as Sojourner Truth, William Lloyd Garrison, Frederick Douglass, Harriet Beecher Stowe, and more. Revolving exhibits take over the center display area, and memorabilia from Anthony's days during the infancy of the women's rights movement are highlighted, including several original copies of *The Revolution,* a newspaper published by Susan B. Anthony and Elizabeth Cady Stanton from 1868 to 1872. Several of Susan's famous quotes are stenciled on the walls ("I am like a snowball. The further I am rolled the more I gain").

I liked this little museum a lot. Colleen Janz is an enthusiastic and able overseer who tends to the history of Anthony's short span of time here in Adams in a loving and sensitive way.

Finally, I asked her if students come to the museum on fieldtrips.

"Well, with the ever tightening of school budgets, a lot of fieldtrips have been discontinued. But that is fine. I pack up my exhibits and take them to the schools, and tell the story to them right in the classroom."

Do they understand the importance of Susan B. Anthony to all of us, particularly young women?

"Yes, they do. One thing I like to do is have the children stand up and read from *The Revolution* newspaper. They don little white gloves, the old-fashioned type that Susan actually wore. It is like they are channeling her in a way. It is heartwarming to see the reaction on their little faces."

The Nuts and Bolts

Susan B. Anthony Birthplace Museum

67 East Road
Adams, Massachusetts 01220
(413) 743-7121
www.susanbanthonybirthplace.org
This museum is handicapped accessible.

Travel Suggestion

This museum is located outside of the downtown business area of Adams. In Susan's day this would have been considered out in the country. Just as you think you have gone too far south on East Road you will arrive at the museum.

Museum Hours

Columbus Day through Memorial Day: Monday, Friday, and Saturday, 10 a.m. to 4 p.m.; Sunday, 11:30 a.m. to 4 p.m.
Memorial Day through Columbus Day: Thursday through Monday, 10 a.m. to 4 p.m.
Private tours can be arranged by calling the museum.

Admission

Adults: $6.00
Seniors: $4.00
Students: $3.00

Up around the Bend

MASS MoCA is in neighboring North Adams. The Massachusetts Museum of Contemporary Arts is located in a wonderfully repurposed, centuries-old brick mill and factory, and it houses one of the largest collections of contemporary and visual arts in the country. MASS MoCA has over 26 buildings with nearly 250,000 square feet of display area. More than 125,000 visitors come here annually.

40 Crane Museum of Papermaking

‿‿‿‿‿‿

Dalton

The Crane & Company sprawls over a campus of aging brick manufacturing buildings tucked in a hillside in Dalton. The company, the oldest paper manufacturer in the country, is a significant presence in this small town, where it employs over 350 people. To get to the company's museum you must follow the signs along a wandering roadway that eventually ends at an attractive stone building. It evokes an English country cottage with its ancient stone walls, beautifully landscaped grounds, quaint marble-based sun dial, and ivy-covered facade. A fading bronze plaque reads, "To commemorate the founding of the first paper mill in Dalton, Massachusetts by Zenas Crane in 1801. Erected by Crane and Company, 1929." This Thomas Kinkade–like apparition looks jarringly out of place among the towering,

sturdy brick workplace buildings of Crane. Surely this little cottage must have a charming, whimsical name to it.

"It was known as the rag room," company historian Peter Hopkins told me.

"Not a very fancy name, for sure, but that is what it was. Tons of rags and strips of cloth were brought in here many years ago, and the rags were then sorted out for imperfections and flaws, and each large piece of cotton or flax was cut by hand into smaller pieces to ready them for literally being beaten to a pulp. The work was almost exclusively done by women, mothers and their daughters."

Hopkins is an affable, walking encyclopedia of the history of this venerable American company. "I never worked here, but I have been involved with this museum for many years. I love the building and the story it tells."

Crane & Company was founded in Dalton in 1801 by Zenas Crane. "Actually, Zenas's father, Stephen, was a papermaker before him. The family took over a mill in the suburbs of Boston in 1770. They left little room for doubt about their desire for independence. They called it the Liberty Paper Mill. Papers from the Liberty Mill were held in high regard, among the finest you could buy. He had some pretty famous customers, too."

With this, Hopkins directed me to a display case along the front wall. "Here is the actual ledger from the first days of the Liberty Paper Mill. If you look down in the far corner you will see a very interesting and very famous name." I looked and there it was for all to see. An order for some paper currency from Paul Revere, dated January 4, 1776. "Revere printed what are called 'Soldier Notes,' used to pay the Massachusetts soldiers for their service in the Revolutionary War. But, as you can see from the order date and the payment date, well, let's just say he was a slow payer," the historian laughed. The payment date is recorded as 1778.

The museum spreads out over the beautifully crafted building designed with arching buttresses overhead and lit by chandeliers. The whole property was referred to as the Old Stone Mill and is itself a building of note. It was designed after the famous Old Ship Church in Hingham, Massachusetts.

"This rag room sat empty for sixty years before it was decided to turn it into a museum in 1929," Hopkins said. "We tell the story of papermaking both in text and in a hands-on way. Down through history the Crane Company became the sterling paper company in the world and our clients are some of the most recognizable names you can imagine."

Hopkins took me to a large set of cases that showcased some examples of Crane's prestigious clients and samples of their purchases. There are Christmas cards printed for President and Mrs. Franklin D. Roosevelt, embossed invitations to the 1937 opening of the Golden Gate Bridge, an RSVP for a concert by presidential daughter Margaret Truman, a wedding invitation to the nuptials of President Johnson's daughter Luci Baines Johnson to Patrick Nugent in 1966, and an embossed invitation to the 1886 dedication of the Statue of Liberty.

"It is a pretty impressive collection. We even made the birthday invitations to the Queen Mother's 100th birthday," he said proudly, as he pointed to a fancily scrolled card with elegant calligraphy printed on it.

Scattered around the large room are archival documents, old photographs, original equipment, and tools that date back to Zenas Crane's founding of the company. And paper. Lots of paper. One thinks of paper as something quite easy to make. Here at Crane & Company they refine the process to an art form.

Early in the Crane timeline, in 1879, the company became the provider of cotton and linen paper to the U.S. Treasury for all of its currency. The company was also a pioneer in advancing techniques to erase counterfeiting, such as watermarking bills and placing colored threads and a range of what are called "optically variable devices" in the currency to thwart criminals. "Of course because of all this, pretty much everything we do inside our manufacturing plant is strictly off-limits to the general public," Hopkins revealed. "Our security is among the tightest you will find in a plant like ours."

I questioned Hopkins on exactly how tight the security was. "Well, let's just put it this way. If you ever wander around the grounds and stand by a tree and wave, you can bet there is a security officer somewhere sitting behind a television console waving back at you," he said.

A favorite part of any tour at the Crane Museum of Papermaking is a large back workroom known as "the garage" where you can actually get up close to the papermaking process. Here, tour guides will let you put your hands in blue-hued goop, made by beating hundreds of scraps of denim into a thick pulp. "We get our denim scraps from Goodwill Industries. They sort them out and cut them up into small pieces, and then we buy them by the twenty-pound bag. Then we turn on the beater wheel and around and around they go until they are pummeled into the consistency of oatmeal. In fact, this used to be done by hand here, and that is where the term 'beaten to a pulp' was born. To make the paper, the pulp is diluted to about 99 percent water and then strained through a fine screen. After gravity is done we apply suction then pressure. What is left is a light blue denim paper ready to go."

Wow Factor

While most people would think the wow factor here has to be the actual ledger with Paul Revere's personal order for currency paper logged into it, the historian has a different take on what thrills him.

"When we take people to the workroom and they watch, up close, the papermaking process in front of them, I like to observe their faces. The process is really interesting for those who have never seen it, and most never have. But the wow factor for me is when we run a wet vac under the strainer. As the visitors watch the water getting sucked out of the strainer, they are actually able to see that magic instant when pulp turns into paper. It is fun to watch the sense of surprise and wonder as it hits them that this is an actual piece of paper that they have just watched being made. I never get tired of that."

The Takeaway

A great asset to the museum is a short video that comes about halfway through the tour. It is an excerpt of a television show called *Made in America* hosted by actor John Ratzenberger. During season four of the hit show, Ratzenberger and his film crew came to Crane to show how paper was made. The film clip is entertaining and informative, and allows the museum visitor to actually see the inside of the manufacturing facility that is off-limits to the general public.

This is one of those little museums that you think is not going to be very interesting (watching paper being made?) but then turns out to be a rewarding experience. The docents are all excellent in their narratives, and historian Peter Hopkins is usually on hand. "I have been here for twenty-seven years," he told me. "I just love it here. I am in a rare position to run a historical museum for a company and a family who is not only relevant in today's world but makes today's world actually work."

The Nuts and Bolts

Crane Museum of Papermaking
40 Pioneer Street
Dalton, Massachusetts 01226
(413) 684-6380
http://www.crane.com/about-us/crane-museum-of
-papermaking
This museum is handicapped accessible.

Travel Suggestion
When you arrive at Crane & Company look for the small
signs to the museum. It is located separate from the
company offices and manufacturing facility. If you set
your GPS to "West Housatonic Street, Dalton, Massachusetts," you will start seeing signs.

Museum Hours
June 2 through the end of October: Monday to Friday,
1 p.m. to 5 p.m.
November 1 through June 1: Tuesday through Thursday,
1 p.m. to 5 p.m.

Admission
Free (and they love kids)

Up around the Bend

Dalton is located just five miles east of Pittsfield. The city of Pittsfield, with a population of over forty thousand, is the largest in
the Berkshires. There are many fine cafes, restaurants, and stores
in the downtown area, and the Berkshire Museum is a renowned
museum featuring fine art, natural history exhibits, and famous
items from great moments in American history (such as artifacts
from the famous Peary/Henson expedition to the North Pole of
1908–9). The museum founder was Zenas Crane.

41 Ventfort Hall Mansion and Gilded Age Museum

~~~

Lenox

They sure don't make them like this anymore.

Ventfort Hall (French for "strong wind") was built in 1893 for George and Sarah Morgan. She was the sister of J. P. Morgan, and she married another Morgan, her seventh cousin. This house, dubbed a "Berkshire cottage" when it was built, consists of nearly thirty thousand square feet of Victorian-era excess: seventeen fire-places, fifty-four rooms, fifteen bedrooms, thirteen bathrooms, plus kitchens and service areas, drawing rooms, billiard rooms, palatial staircases, and a secret safe hidden behind a moveable wall panel outside of Sarah's bedroom.

"We assume she kept her fabulous jewels in there," Linda Rocke told me as she pushed the hidden panel causing it to disappear into the floor and reveal a metal safe. Rocke is the marketing coordinator for the mansion and museum. "This home has a lot of secrets and is such a wonderful place with quite a fascinating history behind it.

A panorama of the Gilded Age is on display here. In fact, it is on display all throughout Lenox. The architect for Ventfort Hall was Arthur Rotch, one of the most famous Boston architects of the era. Five of his splendid mansions were built in Lenox—Ventfort Hall, Thistlewood, Osceola, Belvoir Terrace, and Sundrum. All remain standing today.

"We love this old mansion," Rocke said. "It has great character and beauty. Each room is special in its own way." She guided me in to George Morgan's personal billiard room. It is resplendent with exotic carpets, ornate windows dappled with stained glass, and a magnificent fireplace with towering black mahogany carvings on either side. It has quite a tale behind it. "We believe the Morgans may have 'liberated' this from an old Italian church on one of their many overseas trips," she said. The date on the woodwork surrounding the entry doors says "anno 1630."

Another astounding room is the Great Hall.

"Try and imagine the parties and social events held in this wonderful room," Kelly Blau said as she swept the room with her hand. She is the vice president of the board of directors at Ventfort Hall. "This house doesn't have a ballroom, so this room would have been where they gathered for celebrations and galas." She pointed to a raised portico at the end of the hall. It had a beautiful wood carved balustrade and was backed by curved skylights that let the sunlight in. "That is where the minstrel's gallery would play to entertain the guests," Blau whispered. And on those chilly Berkshire winter evenings, the party would be warmed by the fire roaring in the massive six-ton French limestone fireplace. "It is all original to the building of the mansion," she told me.

After touring the massive home, we strolled out to the ninety-foot-long columned veranda overlooking the back lawn. Here, among wicker arm chairs, Victorian statuary, and overflowing flower urns, it was quite easy to imagine the faces of those coming up from the manicured lawns to enter Ventfort Hall for a ball or dinner. "Yes, this veranda with its view of the property is stunning," Linda Rocke said. "And quite famous, too."

How so, I asked.

"If you have ever seen the Academy Award–winning-film *The Cider House Rules* then you have seen this view from the lawn. In the movie, when you see Michael Caine and Toby McGuire walking up to the orphanage, well, that is us," she laughed.

The Cider House Rules employed this grand lady of a home for exterior shots (where it substituted for the St. Cloud's Orphanage in the film) and used the staircases in the Great Hall for several interior scenes. Ventfort Hall can also be seen in many of the movie's advertising posters.

A billiard room, music rooms, libraries, a drawing room, a great hall for parties, sweeping verandas—just perfect for parties, and I mused that his place must have seen some humdingers in its day. "Oh, most certainly. Remember," Blau said, "This place was built expressly for Sarah Morgan to entertain in. She was an important part of the social circle in Lenox, and her parties were events to really be seen at. And who wouldn't want to come to Ventfort Hall for a soiree?"

I asked both women to share some of the other curious stories about the house and the people who lived here over the decades. Linda Rocke went first. "Ventfort Hall had electric lighting in addition to the traditional gas lighting of the day when it was built.

We have some priceless silver sconces on the walls here. George Westinghouse was one of the Morgans' neighbors right down the street. Mr. Westinghouse put in one of the first residential generators in Lenox, and he 'shared' his electricity with Ventfort Hall."

Wow Factor

"For me it is just the totality of this place as a family residence," Kelly Blau said. "Despite its rambling size I really feel it has a warm, comfortable ambience to it. But it was quite a responsibility running a house of this size. Sarah actually had the letters 'VH' along with a number stitched into the each of the lace linens so they could be properly accounted for," she told me. "She numbered them so she could easily see when the linens were depleted due to indelible stains or tears or just over usage.

"And her initials were sewn into the bed linens, too." And with this we went to look at the white linen coverlet on the bed with Sarah's monogram stitched into it, as well as a tablecloth which read "VH 13." "It was all just a clever way to inventory the hundreds of pieces of linens used here."

Linda Rocke's wow factor was a little different. "There are so many wonderful treasures in this house. I am in awe of all of them. But the stained glass really is my favorite. They spared no expense in buying this glass, and the pieces are remarkable. And so beautiful. The Morgans contracted with the Berkshire Glass Works Company of Lanesborough for many of their windows. The glass company was one of the first such places in America to produce colored stained glass after the Civil War."

The Takeaway

One tends to get numb while visiting one outsized Victorian mansion after the other. This one is a special treat, though, not be missed. It has the benefit of so many different stories all wrapped up in one gigantic, fanciful home. There were surprises virtually around every corner. Look for the fireproof silver safe with a ceramic false ceiling, or those little metal boxes with a wick set inside the wall above the toilets. What were they for? Apparently they served two purposes. The lighted wick served as a nightlight, and they also burned off the methane gas in the unvented bathroom.

"Our mission is to bring the Gilded Age to life through this wonderful residence," Blau said. "This is a house museum, after all. People lived here. Real people. You will find no velvet ropes to stand behind, no 'do not touch' signs. We want to involve people here."

The mansion tells the story of the heyday of Lenox as one of the most well-to-do towns in New England. The property timelines intersect many different chapters of American history. In fact, one of the owners who built the first house on this property had a daughter, Annie Haggerty, who married Colonel Robert Gould Shaw of Massachusetts in 1863. She and Shaw honeymooned at her parent's house, an earlier residence that sat on the site of the present mansion, also called Ventfort. He then went to war and was soon killed while leading his men, the Massachusetts 54th, the first Union regiment of colored troops, in a charge against the enemy at Fort Wagner in Charleston, South Carolina, leaving Annie a widow at only twenty-eight years old. She and her sister sold the property to the Morgans some years later, and the Haggerty house was moved across the street so Ventfort Hall could be built.

The story of Colonel Shaw (played by actor Matthew Broderick) and the Battle of Fort Wagner was told in the 1989 Academy Award–winning film *Glory.*

The Nuts and Bolts

Ventfort Hall Mansion and Gilded Age Museum

104 Walker Street
Lenox, Massachusetts 01240
(413) 637-3206
www.gildedage.org
The first floor is handicapped accessible. Call in advance regarding the second floor, as efforts are underway to add wheelchair accessibility there also.

Travel Suggestion

Ventfort Hall is located just southeast of the downtown business district of Lenox.

Museum Hours

November 1 through Memorial Day: Monday through Friday, 11 a.m. to 4 p.m.; Saturday, 10 a.m. to 4 p.m.; Sunday, 10 a.m. to 3 p.m.
Memorial Day through October 31: Monday through Saturday, 10 a.m. to 5 p.m.; Sunday, 10 a.m. to 3 p.m.

Guided tours are available. Ventfort Hall and the Gilded Age Museum are closed only four days a year: Christmas, New Year's Day, Easter, and Thanksgiving.

Admission

Adults: $18.00
Seniors over 65 and students with ID: $17.00
Children (5–17): $7.00

Up around the Bend

Writer Edith Wharton's magnificent mansion, The Mount, is located just outside of Lenox on Rt. 7. It is open to the public.

Photograph courtesy of AniMagic Museum, www.mambor.com.

42 AniMagic Museum of Animation, Special Effects and Art

 ~~~~~

Lee

This little museum on Main Street in Lee really sticks out. Located in the staid Heaphy 1879 Block building, the museum's two front windows are jammed with dolls, model space ships, costumes, and all sorts of wizardry. The proprietor of the museum is Eugene Mamut. He is a special effects master from Ukraine who has lived in the United States for many years and has lent his talents to a surprising number of top-name Hollywood films. And he has an Academy Award to show for it.

"Yes, this is my award," he told me in his broken English. "I won it on March 30, 1987. It was for my optical camera effects for the movie *Predator.*" In the display case is the actual award resting next to a black-and-white photograph of a much younger Mamut on stage at the Oscars holding his trophy. Curiously, it is not the standard "little gold man" design that we associate with the Oscars. "No, mine was for special effects so the technical award is a little different. But it is an Academy Award, and I am very proud of it."

"Such a big shot," his wife, the Ukrainian artist and sculptor Irina Borisova, chimed in. "Look how handsome he was in his new tuxedo and look at all his hair," she teased.

I asked her what had been the most exciting thing about that special evening. "Oh, meeting the star of the film, Arnold Schwarzenegger. Such a big star, and a big man. But so nice," she smiled.

Eugene and Irina are the custodians of a little-known historical fact. In their small museum, tucked away in the Berkshires, they tell the amazing story of how many of the most talented animators and special-effects wizards in the movie business came to live in this area.

"Douglas Trumbull was the first. He is a genius, of course," Mamut told me. "He lives nearby. He is a special effects magician. He has been in this museum before. He gave the world the wonders of *Star Trek, Blade Runner, 2001: A Space Odyssey, Close Encounters of the Third Kind,* and many other films. His studio is right down the road in Southfield. He was the first great special-effects genius to come to the Berkshires. He wrote and directed the 1972 classic sci-fi film *Silent Running.* Do you know what he named one of the space ships in his movie?" I had no idea. "Well, look here," Mamut said as he pointed to a large movie poster of a "space freighter" from the film. On the side it read, "The Berkshire."

"Doug Trumbull is the sweetest man," Borisova offered. "He is a good friend. He is a true living legend who has worked with all of the greats like Stanley Kubrick, James Cameron, and many others. His work on *Blade Runner* is still the best. You may remember his father, Donald Trumbull? He worked on the special effects in the *Wizard of Oz*. Such a dear man."

"And he won an Academy Award, too," Mamut added.

The *Silent Running* movie poster is just one of many others adorning the walls. All of the films have used the talents of Eugene Mamut and his many "Berkshire animators." He read them off like a wall of honor: *Chicken Run, Wallace and Gromit, Blue Lagoon, Ghost Dad, Dirty Dancing, 9–5, The Chronicles of Narnia,* and others. Mamut earned his everlasting fame in his craft for creating the "camouflage suit," which renders an actor virtually invisible.

"It is all wonderful," he said with a grand sweeping gesture around the museum. "And all of it from right here in the Berkshires. Movies like *Back to the Future, The Lord of the Rings, A Night at the Museum,* all had work done on them in the Berkshires. Did you know that the most sophisticated special effects for the movie *The Matrix,* like the famous slow-motion bullet, were made right here in the Berkshires? Or that Tom Gasek, who did much of the stop-action special effects for *Coraline, Wallace and Gromit,* and *Chicken Run,* did it all right from his studio ten miles from here in Great Barrington? And John Gaeta. He is another genius. He won an Academy Award for special effects for the Robin Williams film *What Dreams May Come.* John is a friend, and lives in the next town up, Lenox. Jeff Kleiser and his wife, Diana Walczak, are up in North Adams. They supervised the special effects for *Spider Man.* And there are many more just like that all throughout the Berkshires."

Even Mamut, the old master that he is, shook his head in amazement.

Wow Factor

"What I never get tired of is playing with the children who come in here," Mamut said. "I say wow every time they leave. They come in, I help them make their own stop-action film out of pieces of clay, I encourage them, and when it is over they jump for joy. It makes my day. Children come in here with 'down faces.' Ugh, a museum of science stuff, they say. But once I get them busy they begin laughing and giggling. It is just such a joyful experience for me. This is not a workplace. It is a play place. I don't want to make money. I want to make smiles. The children ask if they can do this work some day? I tell them I won an Oscar for being an optical effects cameraman. That position doesn't even exist anymore. I tell them the future is all theirs."

"Anything else for a wow factor," I asked?

"Well, you have to admit the Academy Award over on the shelf is pretty amazing, isn't it?" he said with a broad grin.

The Takeaway

This is one of the most unusual museums that I researched for this book. Basically, what you have here are three rooms of a man's (and woman's) life work. Mamut has created many simple, hands-on experiments for visitors to examine. Wheels turn showing cartoon figures running. Black-lights illuminate ghostly faces. Magnets of all kinds do all sorts of magical things. Objects float through the air powered only by static electricity. And, of course, there is the round worktable in the middle.

This is the epicenter of Mamut's world. Adults and kids alike are invited to sit around the table (for a small fee) and make their own clay figures. Then he places these little clay people in a natural setting and begins to film them in stop-action movements. Move an arm an inch here. Move a leg an inch there. And on it goes with Mamut photographing the whole experience. At the end, he puts music behind it all, runs the film in real time, and before their eyes visitors can see their creations. Maybe the next *Gumby?* The next *Mr. Bill?* Probably not, but it is a surefire crowd pleaser every time.

Not to be overlooked at the AniMagic Museum is the contribution of Borisova. She is an award-winning illustrator and sculptor and is herself a master of the art of stop-action filming. A monitor plays a loop of her many familiar television commercials, some of them immediately recognizable even to the casual viewer. Dancing children in a Burger King commercial, singing snowmen in a Hallmark Christmas card spot, happy Claymation shoppers cruising the aisles of Walmart. Especially interesting is a display case filled with all of the finely sculpted characters originally used in these commercials. She is no less a creative genius than her husband.

The Nuts and Bolts

AniMagic Museum of Animation, Special Effects and Art

135 Main Street
Lee, Massachusetts 01238
(413) 841-6679
www.mambor.com
This museum is handicapped accessible.

Travel Suggestion

Do not expect a lot of signs or banners identifying this as a museum. It looks for all the world like an antique store, with its front windows crowded with odd, unusual bric-a-brac (all of it from movies).

Museum Hours

The museum is open every day of the year by appointment, but the owners are generally around; to insure that it is open contact them by phone.

Admission

Free

Up around the Bend

Stockbridge is located just four miles west of Lee. Two "must-sees" in Stockbridge are the Norman Rockwell Museum and the Red Lion Inn, perhaps the most famous inn in Western Massachusetts.